Eye of the Sahara@Plate Tectonics

The Geological Wonders of Plate Tectonics

ANIPE STEEVEN KING
B.Sc.,B.Ed.,M.Div

BLUEROSE PUBLISHERS
India | U.K.

Copyright © Anipe Steeven King 2024

All rights reserved by author. No part of this publication may be reproduced, stored in a retrieval system or transmitted in any form or by any means, electronic, mechanical, photocopying, recording or otherwise, without the prior permission of the author. Although every precaution has been taken to verify the accuracy of the information contained herein, the publisher assume no responsibility for any errors or omissions. No liability is assumed for damages that may result from the use of information contained within.

BlueRose Publishers takes no responsibility for any damages, losses, or liabilities that may arise from the use or misuse of the information, products, or services provided in this publication.

For permissions requests or inquiries regarding this publication, please contact:

BLUEROSE PUBLISHERS
www.BlueRoseONE.com
info@bluerosepublishers.com
+91 8882 898 898
+4407342408967

ISBN: 978-93-6452-815-3

Cover design: Tahira
Typesetting: Tanya Raj Upadhyay

First Edition: October 2024

This book has been dedicated to my parents

Rev. Anipe Rajartatnam
who served the Lord about 40 years and

Smt. Anipe Jeevaratnamma
who worked along with him for the Kingdom of God and now both are in Heavenly glory.

Preface

I am glad to introduce this book" Eye of the Sahara @ Plate Tectonics" as we are going through many assumptions and speculations about the formation of the Eye since its discovery in 1960s by the space observatory. As a continuous researcher and learner I gone through many articles about this structure and watched many videos regarding this issue. I found these assumptions were not accepted by many in my study. I am very much excited why so much of research and discussion about the Saharan desert despite many deserts existed around the globe.

I am thrilled to know that this desert was formed in very little time i.e in a flash!. This sentence dragged my attention and I trust that this geological incident became a major support to my previous title ' Joshua's Long Day @ American Tectonic Plate Movements'. I wish to mention a fact in this book that when the God's servant prayed to stop the Sun in the sky it happened and recorded in the book of Joshua10:12. How the phenomena of Sun stopped in the sky is stopping the rotation of the earth about a day. But it was not happened globally, partial rotation recession was happened in 1405 BC by the American Tectonic Plate Movements towards west against the rotation of the Earth and the Arabian and African plates stand still about a day.

We know when the rotation of the earth stops there should be major geological changes on the face of the earth. A mini dooms day occurred in 1405 BC, because of the unusual speed of South, North American Tectonic Plates towards west, a mega Tsunami started from the Atlantic Ocean deluging the island of Atlantis and devastated the North African lands on the same period. One thing should be remembered that American Tectonic Plates are close to the African continent before 1405 BC. God wants to give final world map to the earth dwellers and He thought of future generation to live without affecting another ice age to European and African Continent. So God moved these tectonic plates and deluged the people of Atlantis (Nephilim) because of their false belief system about the end of the World. He wish to convert this region arid as it was necessary to maintain ecological balance of African Continent and the surrounding countries.

At the same time on a day in 1405 BC, clearly on Joshua's Long Day, while the American Tectonic Plate junctions wide open the lava and magma from the mantle of the earth came out with very high pressure(just like a Inter Continental Ballistic Missile) poured upon a spot in Mauritania creating a structure which later called as Richat Structure and Eye of the Sahara. As per the available information this structure was the effect of neither volcanic activity nor meteorite impact. But the stones found were supporting the volcanic activity. How this circular shape was possible? So it was a geological wonder of the Earth as it was formed at diameter of 40 KMs. This book deals with these issues and how this structure was created with 40KMs diameter. Due to its huge area no one on earth finds it but from the space this was observed by astronauts and revealed to the World. Please go through this book and send your comments to:

Anipe Steeven King VPJ
B.Sc; B.Ed; M.Div
victorprem.vpc@gmail.com
8074871493

Acknowledgements

How joyful it is to write my acknowledgements to a book which reveals a mystery about the geological wonder of the modern World.

I know the author for the last 20 years and he is striving to expand His kingdom through Victory Prayer Centre in Samalkot and in surrounding villages. When I gone through the manuscript, marvel to know how the way he linked up the Biblical history to the geological incidents of the Earth in a systematic way. He gave ample information regarding formation of Eye of the Sahara and answering the speculations about the structure.

It is very interesting to read this book and observing the supporting images included in this book. This book is informative, Biblical and geological. It deals with a subject which is confusing the geologists and scientists.

The Eye of the Sahara was discovered by the astronauts in 1960s but how it was formed is mystery even in this modern world. The author Anipe Steeven King VPJ delve deep into the historical and geological facts to reveal the secrets of formation of this geological wonder 'Eye of the Sahara'. So I recommend this as read worthy.

Rt. Rev. Dr. E.Suvartha Raju
International TV speaker
SAMALKOT

Table of Contents

CHAPTER ONE
Earth and its Creation 1
    What does the Bible teach us about this? 2
    Greek Mythology 2
    Earth Science: Tectonic Plates of the Earth 3
    Boundaries of Tectonic Plates 4
    Why should we learn about Tectonic Plates? 6

CHAPTER TWO
SAHARA and its ORIGIN 7
    Why research on the Sahara Desert? 7
    Traditional Folklore 8
    Smithsonian Magazine 9

CHAPTER THREE
Myth about the formation of the Sahara 11
    Greek Mythology 11
    Phaeton and the Chariot of the Sun 12
    Sahara went from Green to Desert in a flash 17
    Sahara formation time and the consequences 18
    Animal life in Sahara – Prehistoric times 20
    Major Historic Events according to Greek history 20
    The division of history of Sahara 22

CHAPTER FOUR
Sahara's connection to Atlantis 23
    Plate Tectonics 24

CHAPTER FIVE
Earth's Tectonic Plates: Its Movements 31

Key Principles of Tectonic Plate Movements 31
Sea Floor Spreading – subduction of the Plates 32
Structure of the Earth. 36

CHAPTER SIX
Atlantis Deluge @ Joshua's Long Day 41
What did Christian scholars say about the time of demise? 43

CHAPTER SEVEN
Tilt of the Earth 47
Earth's Tilt and its affects 48
What would happen to the Earth if it was not tilted? 50
Would there be any differences at all? 51
What would happen if the Earth stopped rotating for a day? 52

CHAPTER EIGHT
Green Sahara 55
The Sahara Desert used to be a Green Savannah and New
Research Explains Why 56
Earth's Changing Orbit 58
Green Sahara: African Humid Periods Paced by Earth's
Orbital Changes 58
Orbital Forcing of subtropical climate 60

CHAPTER NINE
EYE of the Sahara 61
Mystery of the EYE: 61
Richat Structure by Marie Look March 15, 2024
(Internet-based article)(By the same heading we can come
across this article in Internet) 63
What created the Eye of the Sahara? 64
Composition of the Eye of the Sahara 64
Scientific significance of the Eye of the Sahara 65
The most Amazing Deserts in Africa by Regina Baily: 67

IFLSCIENCE Weekly Newsletter published an article: 69
An article from 'Geographical' by Grace Gourlay
(21 Feb 2024) 72

CHAPTER TEN
Why this devastation? 75
    What if the Sahara had not formed? 76
    Significance of Rock art in Sahara 76

CHAPTER ELEVEN
Radio Carbon dating 78
    When the organic matter subjected to high temperatures,
    how does it affect the carbon dating? 79

CHAPTER TWELVE
Conclusion 81
Bibliography 86
Special Chapter 87

CHAPTER ONE
Earth and its Creation

How wonderful is it, to think about our dwelling place, the Earth! The Earth is a tiny planet revolving around a star among billions of stars in the Universe. It is part of our Solar system, which has the Sun, eight planets, moons, asteroids, and comets. Our Solar system is a part of the Milky Way galaxy. It is one of the billion galaxies in the observable universe. The position of our planet is such that it orbits around the Sun, while the Sun itself is moving within the Milky Way galaxy. It is fascinating to imagine our place in this vast and expanding universe. It is marvelous to contemplate the existence of our planet which is hanging in space and running in its course.

According to current information, the observable Universe with the help of different telescopes is around 93 billion light-years in diameter. This means that the farthest celestial bodies we can observe are about 46.5 billion light-years away from Earth in any direction. However, it is difficult to estimate its exact size as it is expanding as per the scientific studies. The Earth seems to be static but it revolves around the Sun along with its moon and in turn our solar system is travelling along with its neighbours in the Milky Way. If we can draw a graphic for the path of Earth and moon, it is not easily comprehendible by the human brain.

It is pertinent to note that our present understanding and measurements of the size and age of the universe are based on the best available space explorations and observations. We should agree that research and advancements in space technology may refine these estimates in the future. James Webb Telescope is already pushing us to reconsider the existing theories about the origin of the Universe.

What does the Bible teach us about this?

The Bible teaches in the Book of Genesis (Chapters 1 and 2) that the creation of the Earth and Heaven as a divine act of God, the Creator. It explains that in the beginning God created the Heavens and the Earth. This states that a sequence of events over the course of six days took place and hence, the entire creation came into existence. God brings forth light, separates the waters to create the sky and sea, and forms the dry land and produces green vegetation. On the fourth day, God creates the Sun, and the Moon, the Stars to govern the night. The Bible further states that on the fifth day, God fills the sky and sea with living creatures like birds and fish. On the sixth day, God creates land animals and ultimately creates human beings in his own image. The creation of Body, Soul and Spirit. The Book of Genesis emphasises not only the creation of the Earth but also of all living beings. Some space explorers may think that Bible account did not give sufficient details about the creation. However the author believes that God gave the information about the Universe based on what extent humans could understand in those days.

The phrase 'Heavens…. Earth' means the Hebrew way of expressing totality. God showed special interest in creating humans in his own image and likeness. God's image in us gives us the ability to reason and the power of understanding His mighty works on this Earth.

The creation account was not meant to be a scientifically proven act but rather a primary witness to the profound truth of God, the creator. As the creator who takes care of us, challenges to be responsible stewards of the gift of life and the nature he provided to us.

Greek Mythology

According to Greek mythology, the creation of the Earth is explained in various myths and assumptions. One of the most popular versions is found in Hesiod's Theogony. In the beginning, there was chaos, a formless and empty void. Then Chaos led to the emergence of Gaia (the Earth) and other deities like Eros (God of Love), Tartarus (God of the Underworld), and the Abyss (part of the underworld). Gaia then gave birth to Uranus, the God of Sky who became his companion and Ruler of the Heavens. Gaia and Uranus became the parents of the Titans, Cyclopes and Hecatoncheires, among other offsprings. The Titans were powerful beings who became the first divine rulers. Greek Mythology ,in this regard, highlights the emergence of the Earth from Chaos, the birth of the gods and their struggle for power. It is imperative to note that Greek mythology includes multiple variations of creation myths, as different regions and authors contributed their interpretations and stories to the rich tapestry of Greek mythology.

Earth Science: Tectonic Plates of the Earth

The Earth's Lithosphere is divided into several large Tectonic Plates. These plates are massive sections of the Earth's crust that move and interact with each other. Some of the major Tectonic Plates are:

1. Pacific Plate
2. North American Plate
3. South American Plate
4. African Plate
5. Eurasian Plate
6. Australian Plate
7. Antarctic Plate
8. Indian Plate

The Plates interact with each other at their boundaries, which can be divided as:

Convergent- coming together

Divergent- moving apart

Or Transform- (sliding past each other). These interactions contribute to various geological phenomena such as earthquakes, volcanoes, and the formation of mountain ranges.

Graphic 01:(Tectonic plate boundaries of the Earth have to include. To highlight the four junctions i.e South, North, and Eurasian, African Plates in the Atlantic Ocean)

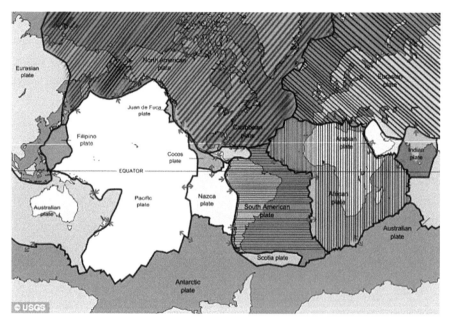

Tectonic plate divisions of the Earth

Boundaries of Tectonic Plates

The boundaries of tectonic plates are dynamic zones whose significant geological events and notable geological features occur.

Subduction Zones: When an oceanic plate collides with a continental plate the denser oceanic plate is forced beneath the continental plate in a process called subduction. For example, the Nazca plate (oceanic plate) in the above picture collides with the South American continental plate. The oceanic plate is completely under water and the continental plate is a land mass sometimes it is a land mass and water. This can lead to the formation of deep-sea trenches, volcanic arcs, and earthquakes. The subduction zone along the western coast of South America is the best example of this case.

Rift zones: In divergent boundaries where plates move apart are called rift zones. These areas can be marked by the emergence of mid-ocean ridges or rift valleys on land. The best example of a mid-ocean ridge is the Atlantic ridge which diverged only in the recent past. The term Great Rift Valley is most often used to the valley of the East African Rift, the divergent plate boundary which extends from Afar Triple Junction southward through eastern Africa, and is in the process of splitting the African Plate into two new and separate plates.

Transform Boundaries: A transform boundary or conservative boundary is where two tectonic plates slide alongside each other. When this happens, the scraping of the two plates causes earthquakes. The San Andreas Fault in California is a well-known transform boundary.

Mountain Ranges: The collision of two continental plates can lead to the formation of large mountain ranges. The Himalayas are a prominent example, formed by the collision between the Indian Plate and the Eurasian Plate. Fold Mountains are created where two or more of Earth's tectonic plates are pushed together, often at regions known as convergent plate boundaries and continental collision zones. The Cape Fold Mountains of South Africa were formed when the ancient Falklands Plateau crashed into the African plate.

Volcanic Islands: Hotspots, which are plumes of magma rising from deep within the Earth. These areas can cause volcanic activity at specific points within the tectonic plate. This can result in the formation of volcanic islands like Hawaii which is situated on the Pacific plate.

Why should we learn about Tectonic Plates?

To understand the formation of the Sahara Desert it is essential fact to know about the tectonic plates. Sahara formation is one massive Act of God or nature in the history of mankind. In the coming chapters, you will know about the intriguing aspect of the Sahara and the formation of the Eye of the Sahara and its link with the movement of Tectonic plates in the mid-Atlantic Ocean. Be patient in this journey of knowing a mystery. The above are just a few examples of the diverse geographical features and events that occur at the boundaries of tectonic plates. The interactions between these plates shape the Earth's surface and contribute to the dynamic nature of our planet.

It is noteworthy that South, the North American Tectonic plates, the African, and Eurasian Tectonic plates have their junctions in the Atlantic Ocean. At a point in time, the junctions wide open and South, North American Tectonic Plates travelled westward with unusual speed and caused great devastation on North African fields which will be explained in the coming chapters.

CHAPTER TWO

SAHARA and its ORIGIN

It is essential to know about the deserts on Earth before 1405 BC. There are many deserts around the World besides the Sahara. In the Bible, the desert of Sin, the desert of Sinai, the desert of Cades and the Desert of Paran are mentioned. Some notable deserts exist on the Earth and their areas in sq. kilometres:

Name of the Desert	Location	Area in Sq. Kilometers
Arabian Desert	Arabian Peninsula	2,000,000
Godi Desert	Asia	804,672
Mojave Desert	South America, Chile	65,983
Great Sandy Desert	Western Australia	150,000
Arctic Polar Desert	South Pole, frigid wasteland	14.2 million

Why research on the Sahara Desert?

Image -03 showing entire Sahara desert

Besides the above deserts that existed from ancient times, lot of research and speculations about the formation of the Sahara Desert. There was a notable variation between the formation of the above deserts and the Saharan Desert. It is quite different from above mentioned deserts. We should be grateful and thankful to the geologists and explorers who wandered in arid conditions in the Sahara Desert bringing out valuable data from sites with great commitment and hard work. Some of them spent their own funds to explore the Sahara.

Traditional Folklore

According to folklore, different cultures have their own explanations for the formation of the Sahara Desert. These explanations often vary and can be influenced by local beliefs and cultural interpretations. It is important to note that these oral traditions may not align with scientific explanations. From the below, we learn more about which tribe believed what regarding the Sahara:

The story of Asibi people: In some Tuareg traditions, there is a story about a Woman named Asibi who transformed the land into a desert. Asibi was said to possess magical powers and was angered by the actions of her people. In her fury, she caused the once fertile land to dry up, resulting in the formation of the Sahara Desert.

The tale of the Dogon people: According to the Dogon people of Mali state that their legend that tells the story of the creation of the Sahara Desert. The tradition of these people tells us that the desert was formed when their ancestors drained a large lake and caused the land to become arid.

These traditional tales and legends serve as cultural explanations and interpretations of the natural landscapes, incorporating legends and mythical elements to explain the formation of the Sahara Desert. They may provide insights into the beliefs and customs of different communities.

The story of the Sahara was passed through the oral tradition means that the formation of the Sahara is near past and not millions of years ago. One scientist reveals that as little as 5,000 years ago, the vast Sahara Desert was covered in grasslands that received plenty of rainfall but shifts in the World's weather patterns abruptly transformed the vegetated region into some of the driest lands on Earth.www.weform.org in the World Economic Forum states " As recently as 5,000 years ago, one of the world's driest and most uninhabitable places, the Western Sahara desert, was home to a vast river system that would rank as the world's largest drainage basin if it existed today.

Why the Sahara formation comes down from millions of years to the near past is explained in the next chapters. So, I (the author) am requesting you to delve into the facts that the author going to present before you.

While cultural legends and oral traditions may not always align with scientific explanations, they play a vital role in shaping people's understanding of natural phenomena, providing cultural context, emotional connections, and moral guidelines that contribute to their worldview and relationship with the natural world.

Smithsonian Magazine

Lorraine Boissoneault states that in her (She is researcher and article writer) article "What Really Turned the Sahara Desert from a Green Oasis into a Wasteland?" (An article in Smithsonian magazine, March 24, 2017)

"The Sahara has long been to periodic bouts of humidity and aridity. These fluctuations are caused by slight wobbles in the tilt of the Earth's orbital axis, which in turn changes the angle at which solar radiation penetrates the atmosphere. At repeated intervals throughout Earth's history, there's been energy pouring in from the seen during the West Africa monsoon season, and during those times known as African Humid Periods- much more rain down over North Africa.

With more rain, the region gets more greenery and rivers and lakes. All this has been known for decades. But between 4,500 and 8,000 years ago, something strange happened; the transition from humid to dry happened far more rapidly in some areas we know today." Scientists usually call it 'power parameterization' of the data, "Wright said by email. "Which is to say that we have no idea what we're missing here- but something wrong"?

Here the author partially agrees with the article by Lorraine and the sudden devastation was much earlier, as she mentions 2,500 BC. But the author establishes much latest part, the green Sahara changes into sand dunes and the mountains that existed in North Africa were suddenly destroyed by sea water and fire which poured like rain on most parts of North Africa. The author discloses the exact year of devastation and sudden catastrophic events that caused the green land to the present state of devastation. You are requested to continue your journey of reading the book until the mystery is revealed.

CHAPTER THREE

Myth about the formation of the Sahara

Myth: A myth refers to a traditional story or narrative that typically originates from ancient cultures or societies. Myths often involve gods, goddesses, supernatural beings, heroes and other elements of the supernatural or divine.

Myth serves various purposes within a culture including explaining natural phenomena. It portrays moral lessons and preserves cultural traditions and beliefs. It provides a framework for understanding the World. They are deeply intertwined with the cultural identity and worldview of a particular community. Myths may be based on historical events with symbolic and metaphorical elements that go beyond literal interpretations. It is important to note that myths can vary significantly between cultures. They may be orally transmitted or depicted through visual arts and performances. Regardless of their form, myths are an integral part of the human storytelling tradition and continue to fascinate and captivate audiences to this day.

Greek Mythology

Greek mythology refers to the collection of myths and legends that originated in ancient Greece. It has its origins in the prehistoric period and developed further during the classical periods of Greek history. The exact time period of Greek mythology can be difficult to pinpoint as it has evolved over centuries.

The earliest forms of Greek mythology can be traced back to the Bronze Age around 1200 BC. The archaic period which lasted from 800 BC to 500 BC in which the development of significant myths and the emergence of important cults and religious practices. This period witnessed the rise of Athens and Sparta and the establishment of various pan- Hellenic religious festivals such as the Olympic Games.

When we observe Greek mythology and its development the Sahara Desert formation might be preceded to 1200 BC. Greek mythology started around 1200 BC and the story of Phaethon scorching the North African lands reveals the Sahara Desert formation is in the near past and it should be near to the pre-historic period and it can be passed through oral tradition. Therefore, let us go through the myth of Phaethon to understand this mystery.

Phaeton and the Chariot of the Sun

By James Parks & Sally Corbett

In ancient Ethiopia, there lived a young man (lad) by the name of Phaeton. His mother was an Ethiopian princess but Phaeton's father was the sun-God himself. One day Phaeton was playing with a friend he boasted that his father was Apollo, the sun-God. Phaeton's friend teased him by saying "Your father really isn't the Sun. Your mother just made that up and you are foolish to believe such a story"

Graphic 02: Chariots of Phaethon and the images of destruction in the North African region.

Phaeton went home confused and ashamed. He told his mother of the taunt and begged her to give him some proof that he really was the child of the Sun. His mother spoke softly but proudly, "My son, your father truly is the radiant Sun. But if you have doubts, then why not go to his palace and speak to him yourself? Go to the far East and there, in the high mountains you will find the glittering palace of your father, the Sun"

Phaeton was overjoyed at his mother's answer which made him ready for the long journey. He travelled in the land of Persia and crossed the strange land of India. Finally, he came to the gigantic mountains at the eastern end of the world. The boy climbed into the mountains and found a palace that he immediately knew must belong to Apollo. Although it was early in the morning and still dark, this tall palace of gold and bronze glowed like fiery coals. The entrance of the palace was through two huge gleaning silver doors. On these doors were carved intricate details of the gods and creatures of the world.

The boy walked through the doorway and came upon a dazzling sight. There stood a golden-haired young woman dressed in a bright green robe. She was covered with flowers that had been braided into her long yellow hair. Nearby was a dark-haired woman dressed in emerald green, holding an armful of golden grain. Beside her was a man with auburn hair and dressed in a robe of orange, yellow and red leaves. His hands were stained purple and he held a cluster of freshly harvested grapes. Last of all was an old man whose bluish-white hair and beard looked like icicles. These were the four seasons and they stood in a half circle around the brilliant throne. It hurt Phaeton's eyes to gaze at this throne, for it was made of shimmering jewels and upon his throne, sat Apollo. The god's eyes blazed like fire and the crown on his head seemed to be made of pure radiant light.

Apollo spoke," Why have you come here to the far ends of the earth, Phaeton?"

The boy replied, "Sir, I have come to find proof that you, great Apollo, are truly my father."

The Sun-God smiled and answered, "Your mother has spoken the truth. I am your father. As proof of this, I will grant your one wish of your heart's desire."

No sooner had Apollo spoken when Phaeton blurted out, "I wish to drive your chariot, father."

The god of light quickly regretted giving his child a wish and pleaded "No, my child, choose something else. You ask for too dangerous of a gift. Even Zeus, the mighty god of thunder, will not drive the chariot of the Sun. The horses breathe out flames and the chariot itself is fiery hot. So powerful are the steeds that I can barely restrain them. What chance would a mortal boy have? The journey is steep and at times I have grown dizzy looking down from the great height of the Earth below. The path through the stars leads to great, dangerous creatures. You would have to pass Taurus, the giant bull, and the fierce lion. If you succeed in getting past them you will face the Scorpion with its huge deadly stinger and the pinching claw of the great Crab. I beg you to pick some other gift. Think of all the riches in the world or pearls from the bloodless sea. Ask for any of these and I shall gladly give it to you."

But Phaeton refused to change his mind and insisted on driving the chariot of the Sun. Apollo sighed and led the boy to the magnificent chariot. It was made of blazing gold, with golden wheels that had spokes of silver. The chariot was embedded with rubies and other precious gems. But unlike Earthly jewels, these gave off a dazzling glow. The horses were called and then brought forth by the Hours, goddesses who waited upon the sun.

At the time Aurora, Goddess of the Dawn, opened the curtains of her splendid palace and, the skies were filled with a rosy glow.

The sun-God spoke," It is almost time for the chariot to begin its daily course. But there is still time for me to take your place. Heed my plea and let me go forth, my son."

But he still wanted to have his heart's desire. So, his father anointed Phaeton's head with magic oil and then placed the crown of light on the boy's head. Then he gave instruction, "Do not use the whip on the horses, my child, for the stallions have enough energy to speed forward on their own. That will be the safest for you and give the Earth the proper light and heat.

The glow from Aurora's palace had now turned golden and the morning star had set. Thus, the day beckoned the horses of the Sun who were pawing the ground and letting to blasts of fiery flames with each snort, with a bolt, they charged forth. But their load was much lighter than what they were used to, so these steeds ran faster and wilder than usual.

Poor Phaeton was terror-stricken and could barely hold the reins much less restrain the powerful horses. Higher and higher the stallions went and thus the rays of the Sun chariot grew distant from the Earth. The sky turned black as night, with the Sun only as a speck of light far above. The horses of the sun ran towards the pole star and in doing so came near the giant serpent. This serpent for ages had been sluggish and harmless since it was in the icy-cold regions of the pole star. But now the great heat from the sun chariot awoke the horrible snake and it hissed, exhaling poisonous breath.

As Phaeton looked down from the great height, his head grew dizzy and he felt sick in his stomach. With the furious horses of fire running madly before him, Phaeton wished he had never set foot in his father's chariot. Now the chariot was speeding head-long toward the gigantic scorpion. The huge monster raised its tail in an attempt to slash out with its stinger. The fear-struck boy completely dropped the reins and the unchecked horses galloped downwards.

Closer and closer the fiery chariot came to the Earth. Rivers began to dry up, and cities and forests caught fire because of the great heat. Neptune raised his head from the sea and shook his trident angrily at the chariot of the sun. But the air was so hot that Neptune soon dove back into the deep blue sea.

As the chariot crossed the continent of Africa it was so close that it set on fire the great Sahara Forest. That wooded region of Northern Africa was reduced to ashes and burning sands. (impression added)

All creatures began to cry to Zeus for help because of the unbearable heat. The gods, the humans, the animals, and the Earth herself were afraid that everything would soon be burned up. Zeus listened to their plea and then he climbed on high. He was armed with a thunderbolt and he threw the deadly shaft at the chariot of the sun. The magic oil Apollo had put on Phaeton protected the boy from the heat and the flames of the chariot, but it could not save him from a thunderbolt of Zeus. There was a deafening crash as the lightning shattered the chariot and Phaeton fell wrapped in sizzling flames. The horses ran home when pieces of the wrecked chariot fell hissing into the sea.

Quickly the master craftsman of the Gods, Vulcan, made a new golden chariot for the sun. But Apollo was so sad over his son's death that he refused to drive it. So, the next day passed without sunlight (one day passed without sun is noteworthy because of this catastrophe there was no light for a day in this region). Zeus and the other gods then came and pleaded with Apollo, begging him not to leave the world in darkness, the Sun-God grieved bitterly of his son's death at the hand of Zeus.

But the chief of Gods replied,

"You have lost a son, true. But how many men on Earth were burned up? I had no choice but to blast the fiery chariot, otherwise every creature on Earth would have been destroyed."

With these words and those of the other gods, Apollo was finally persuaded to return to his rightful duty. He bridled his fiery horses to the Sun chariot the next day the Sun once again travelled its correct course. It still gives proper light and heat to this very day. (This is the end of James Parks & Sally Corbett's article)

Why the author choose this article from the internet? This myth reveals the truth that the Northern African lands were destroyed in a single day but not millions of years to form this land of nothing. This Greek myth was passed to the historical period of African history meaning that it must be happened in the near past but not certainly millions of years ago. Thank you all for reading this Greek myth in order to understand my claim of the Sahara Desert formation.

The above myth reveals the truth that North African lands scorched suddenly and great devastation occurred in the Northern part of the African continent. The author believes and gives further details of the facts about the Saharan desert and its formation. Some scientific researchers propose that the Green Sahara turned into sandy Sahara in a flash i.e. within a day. Here in this mythical story the course of a day the North African lands were devastated and became desert in very little time relatively. The author proposes a single day and night for the formation of the Sahara supernaturally.

Sahara went from Green to Desert in a flash

(An article found on the Internet from the site 'Live Science's Our Amazing Planet) www.ouramazingplanet.net

"From lakes and grasslands with hippos and giraffes to a vast desert, North Africa's sudden geographical transformation 5,000 years ago was one of the planets' most dramatic climate shifts.

The transformation took nearly simultaneously across the continent's northern half, a new study finds. The result will appear in an upcoming issue of the Journal Earth and Planetary Science Letters.

The findings come from analyses of dust blown west from Africa and dropped into the Atlantic Ocean. Researchers sifted through 30,000 years of dust and ocean bottom mud retrieved with ocean drilling ships. The changing levels of windblown dust in the ocean sediments provide scientists with clues to Africa's climate and how it has changed over time. Simply, a lot of dust means drier conditions and less dust means a wetter environment.

The wet period, called the African Humid Period (AHP), started and ended suddenly, confirming previous studies by other groups, of the sediments. However, toward the Humid Period's end about 6,000 years ago, the dust was at about 20 percent of today's level, for less dusty then, previous estimates, the study found.

The study may give scientists a better understanding of how changing dust levels relate to climate by providing inputs for climate models, David McGee, an MIT paleoclimatology and lead study author, said in a statement. Sahara Desert dust dominates modern-day ocean sediments off the African coast and it can travel in the atmosphere all the way to North America.

McGee and his colleagues are now testing whether the dust measurements can resolve a long-standing problem: the inability of climate models to reproduce the magnitude of wet condition in North Africa 6,000 years ago".

Sahara formation time and the consequences

The author agrees that the Sahara formed green to desert in a flash. It is important to note that tectonic plate movements and Earth's tilt support the cause of sudden change in North African lands. Particularly in the pre-historic period there was global devastation and particularly in North African lands, Tsunamis and fire from the sky fell on this region in a massive way as the North, South American Tectonic Plates having junctions with Eurasian and African Plates under the island of Atlantis vide open deluging Atlantis. Here it is pertinent to know plate tectonics and its movements. The subduction (going into the mantle of the Earth) of Nazca and Cocos Tectonic plates took place. In the inner Earth, the net volume of the liquid lava increased suddenly the lava and the sand in the mantle came out with great force and just like a projectile the lava poured on a particular place in the region of Mauritania. The opening up of the Tectonic Plates in the Atlantic Ocean caused this devastation and the generation at that time assumed that the Sun lost its routine route and scorched the North African lands. But the fact is, due to massive movements of North, South American Tectonic plates, a great Tsunami from the Atlantic Ocean devastated the land in an unprecedented way, which is difficult to perceive by the human mind. The time of devastation that led to the Sahara formation is a puzzle from the centuries. The author of this book believes that the solution is to understand the plate tectonics and if we are ready to accept the truth about the geological incident that occurred in the history of Earth and mankind. The author suggests that before 1405 BC, the North African Lands were lush green with savannahs, probably not highly populated too.

The rainfall of the land prior to 1405 BC was very high and floods were very common in these regional rivers. The author states that these greenwood lands and green mountain ranges attract the cool waves that came from the North Pole and Europe made the region wet always. These continuous monsoons may cause the rivers to flood continuously disturbing the ecological balance of the region. This might have led to another Ice Age in the North African region and very severe cold conditions in the entire European continent. So, this issue should be dealt with supernaturally to safeguard the ecological balance of the entire region.

When we delve into the ecological history of the Earth, before 1405 BC, many deserts existed, to maintain the ecology of certain regions. There should be arid conditions in this part of the globe, so the supernatural activity initiated in this region by turning this green land into a hot Sahara in the near past.

Animal life in Sahara – Prehistoric times

During the prehistoric period, the Sahara was not an arid desert as it is today. Instead, it was a much more hospitable environment with a diverse range of animal life. Hence are some examples of animal life that existed in the Sahara during prehistory times:

TYPES OF SPECIES (Pre-historic times)	ANIMALS and SPIECES EXISTED
Megafauna	African Elephant, Barbary Lion, cape Buffalo and Hippopotamus
Herbivores	Species like Giraffe, various antelopes, scimitar-horned Oryx, etc
Carnivores	Lions, cheetahs, hyenas, foxes and wolves
Aquatic	Fish, turtles, crocodiles and various waterfowl
Reptiles	Snakes, lizards, tortoises and Nile crocodiles

It is important to note that animal life in the prehistoric Sahara varied over time, with shifts in climate and environment leading to changes in species composition. As the region transformed into an arid desert, we know today, that many species either migrated or became extinct resulting in a significant loss of biodiversity in the Sahara.

Major Historic Events according to Greek history

In Greek history, the historic period is typically considered to have begun with the emergence of written records and the development of the Greek alphabet. This period is often referred to as the classical period which spans from the 500 BC to the death of Alexander the Great in 323 BC.

During this period, the Greeks made significant contributions to various fields including philosophy, literature, art, politics and warfare. Greek history is known for the rise and dominance of Athens and Sparta as well as the golden age of Athenian democracy and intellectual progress. Some important events and figures from the historic period in Greek history include:

The Key Events in Greece	Time or Period	Name of the Battle/
The Persian War	499 BC	Battle of marathon, battle of Thermopylae, battle of Salamis
The Peloponnesian war	421-404 BC	War of Sparta

The Golden age of Pericles (461- 429 BC): A period of cultural and artistic advancements in Athens under the leadership of Pericles marked by the construction of iconic buildings like the Parthenon on the Acropolis.

Prominent Philosophers: The historic period saw the emergence of influential Greek philosophers including Socrates, Plato and Aristotle who laid the foundations of Western Philosophy.

Alexander the Great (356-323 BC): The historic period in Greek history concludes with the conquests of Alexander the Great transforming the Greek world into a vast empire that stretched from Greece to Egypt and India.

These are just a few examples of the significant events and figures from the historical period in Greek history. The author wish to mention the historic period of Greek because, the third century philosopher, Plato, mentioned an ancient city Atlantis and its deluge in his writings Timaeus and Critias. And also the story of Sahara mentioned in Greek mythology which reveals a story how the North African lands scorched by Phaeton who led the Sun's chariot in a wrong route. This myth clearly mentioned the scorching of the North African lands during this time. The literature and writing started in Greece roughly about 500 BC, so the event of scorching the earth should be happen evidently near past to 500 BC. There is no chance to come down the story to Greek history by oral tradition if it happened millions of years ago. This should pass by oral tradition among Greeks from the near past to their historical recordings of various Greek texts. So the author divides the history of the Sahara as follows:

The division of history of Sahara

The author divides the history of the Sahara as before 1405 BC and after 1405 BC. Why this point is taken as base will be explained clearly in the coming chapters. The official records of Greek history started in 500 BC. Thus, if we want to analyse the reasons for how and when the Sahara formed should be dealt with very carefully.

Graphic 04: Timeline of Sahara Formation

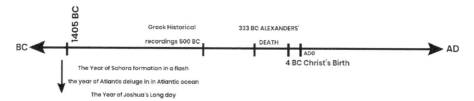

In 1405 BC, major geological incidents occurred due to the movements of tectonic plates deluging the great ancient city Atlantis in the Atlantic Ocean in a single day and night. This incident had a link with Sahara Desert's formation because, the junctions of four tectonic plates under Atlantis were open and this island was deluged and mixed with lava erupted from the junctions. The author strongly believes that this is the doomsday of the near past in order to regulate the temperatures of the Earth as if now. So, the readers have to know about the Tectonic Plates movements in order to know what devastation occurred on the Northern part of Africa and how a great island deluged in a single day and night. This is the key point of this book and you will certainly marvel at the conclusion of this book.

CHAPTER FOUR

Sahara's connection to Atlantis

As we go through the speculations and mythical records from Greek history, we may come to a conclusion that Atlantis was not a real place, because there were no archaeological and historical records about Atlantis, that's why this city called as mythical.

But as the 3rd Century BC philosopher stated that Atlantis was a real place and it was the size of Libya and Asia Minor together. The author of this book gave clear explanation in his previous book "Joshua's Long Day @ American Tectonic Plate Movements" which is available on the Amazon app.

Atlantis is assumed to be an island that existed in Atlantic Ocean just opposite the present Pillars of Hercules at the Strait of Gibraltar. It is author's hypothesis that present island Azores in the Atlantic Ocean is the remnant of Atlantis Island after the devastation. Plato stated that the big continent was deluged in Atlantic Ocean in a single day and night. This statement inspired the author to investigate this island.

Generally, the volcanic activity starts slowly and lasts in months; in some cases it takes years except in case of Pompeii. But the case is not the same with Tectonic Plate Movements. The geologists always taking into consideration, the present speed of tectonic plates which is very low. But at some times by supernatural intervention this speed might be thousands of kilometres per day. The author of this book will explain how and when it was occurred in the coming chapters. In the creation account God gathered the waters to one place means the Tectonic Plates moved to one place and the waters went to downward. This was creation act of God done within 24 hours. The Tectonic Plate Movements occurred before the mankind even hardly knew that the Earth was created with many tectonic plates and existed as spherical ball in this universe. We can't explain divine acts with scientific proofs. The Red Sea was divided supernaturally and it was a divine act. Science can't explain how the waters stood as walls on both sides.

Earth is a marvellous and beautiful planet created by God, specially created for the inhabitation of his loved children, human beings. On the surface of the earth, we have many minerals, rivers and oceans and ice glaciers. This is the outward view of the Earth. But there is a more complicated structure inside it. To understand the sudden demise of Atlantis in a single day and night, we must understand the Plate Tectonics of the Earth.

Plate Tectonics

The author believes that in no other star system would we find another planet like ours, if it was not planned and created by God. When we see it from the space, we can see it as a green ball with clothed with a white and blue robe. But that is the external view, let us take a look at Earth internally.

To understand the North and South American Tectonic plate movements to the present positions during Joshua's Long Day or Atlantis deluge, we should have minimum knowledge about the plate tectonic theory which describes the large- scale motions of Earth's lithosphere. The plate movements means millions of tonnes of matter being moved by the inner force of the Earth.

Graphic 05: showing Lithosphere and asthenosphere inside the Earth.

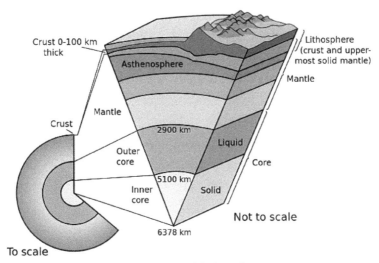

Layers of the Earth & Earth's interior structure

The lithosphere (outer layer of the Earth) is broken up into tectonic plates. On Earth, there are seven or eight major plates (depending on how they are defined) and many minor plates. Where plates meet, their relative motion determines the type of boundary: convergent, coming together (pacific and African plates), divergent, moving away from each other (North and South American plates) or transforming (east Pacific rise and Mid-Atlantic Ridge). Earthquakes, volcanic activity, mountain- building, and oceanic trench (deep depressions) formation occur along these plate boundaries. Generally lateral relative movement of the plates typically varies from zero to 100 mm annually.

But the North and South American plates moved apart with high speed against the rotational speed of the earth by the conventional currents occurred in the outer part of the mantle. The theory of viscosity also helped these plates to move at high speed.

Tectonic plates are composed of oceanic lithosphere and thicker continental lithosphere, each topped by its own kind of crust. Along convergent boundaries, subduction carries plates into the mantle; the material lost is roughly balanced by the formation of new (oceanic) crust along divergent margins by seafloor spreading. (We must understand that the ocean floor between Atlantic ridge and shores of North and South American contents were newly formed i.e. before 1405 BC). In this way, the total surface of the globe remains the same. This prediction of plate tectonics is also referred to as the Conveyor Belt Principle. This means some plates subduct into the earth and molten lava comes out as seafloor spreading as in the case Atlantic ridge along the South and North American Tectonic plate junctions.

Tectonic plates can move because the Earth's lithosphere has a higher strength and lower density than the underlying asthenosphere. Lateral density variations in the mantle result in convection. Plate movement is thought to be driven by a combination of the motion of the seafloor away from the spreading ridge (due to variations in topography and density of the crust, which result in differences in gravitational forces) and drag downward suction, at the subduction zones. Another explanation lies in the different forces generated by the rotation of the globe and tidal of the Sun and Moon. The relative importance of each of these factors is unclear, and is still subject to debate".

We have gone through the Earth's inner structure and how the Tectonic plates moved supernaturally deluging the island Atlantis in a single day and night. Let me conclude how the Sahara formed in a flash. The junctions of four Tectonic Plates happened to be under the island of Atlantis (the present-day Azores Island in North Atlantic ocean, the author believes that Azores island is the remnant of Atlantis) and the South and North American Tectonic Plates travelled westward in the near past. A massive Tsunami occurred as the Tectonic Plates began to move destroyed North African lands, at the same time along the junctions between African Plate and North,

South American Plates open. As the North American plate travelled westward the Nazca and Cocos minor plates in Pacific Ocean submerged into the mantle of the Earth with enormous amounts of sand and soil. The inner volume in mantle of the Earth increased suddenly and at the same time tilting of the Earth towards east happened. Hence, huge amounts of the hot sand and soil came out of the junctions and poured into North African lands in a massive way. The human mind cannot perceive the act of God pouring the millions of tonnes of sand with fire on North African lands devastating the entire region as the land of nothing. Even when it comes to the 'Eye of the Sahara' formation in the near past, the modern civilization came to know about it from space only during 1960s. We know that 50 km radius of the Eye of the Sahara is one of the biggest natural phenomena ever found on the face of the Earth.

Recently, the satellite images revealed the fact about fresh water lakes, green savannahs, and woodlands under the sands of Sahara. The author claims that formation of Sahara happened in a flash and it was a day in the near past.

Graphic 06: "The lava poured upon a spot in Mauritania just like a projectile and hot sand poured upon North African region."

Just like a submarine to surface missile in warfare, the sand and fire poured on the African lands devastating the mountain ranges and the forests in North Africa. It is evident fire on the mountain ranges of North Africa as the highest mountains also seemed to be scorched by heat and nothing green was left over on the mountains. As the author of this book already mentioned that a great Tsunami, which was not experienced by modern society, occurred on that day, the Sea water drained to the highest and lowest parts of the North African lands along with some aquatic species like big fish of the Atlantic Ocean. The recent fossil record reveals the same to us. This is the reason some geologists found salt deposits in the highest points and lowest of the lands. As per the author's assumption that when tectonic plates moves the Tsunami started, as the tsunami takes time, fire and sand came out of the centre of four Junctions under Atlantis, and liquid lava came out from the mantle the Earth and poured upon a spot in Mauritania. This results to create a concentric circle-like structure on a particular point in Mauritania formed. The liquid lava poured upon this spot in a massive way.

As shown in the above image the Tectonic plate junctions vide open and the North, and South American tectonic plates travelled westward with unusual speed. From the junctions of these plates the fire came out the enormous amount of sand projected from the Atlantic Ocean and fell on the North African region in a single day and night. This was a semi-doomsday in the prehistoric period. As mentioned earlier in the mythical story of Phaeton a truth of scorching the North African lands recorded. Down from this pre-historic period, this story was passed down through Oral traditions and poetical imaginations wrote the truth through a Greek myth.

Shall we be against the scientific outcomes of the carbon-14 dating? No, not at all. But we should remember that materials that have accurate dates, are important. Carbon formed on the Sahara lands is definitely exposed to severe heat and moreover the material deposited on the surface is from the mantle of the earth. The particles that may deposit on the carbon particles of the fossils belong to the time of millions of years as the Earth and the inner matter existed from the beginning. The Earth was existed first as Pangaea and then by the Tectonic Plates moved just like an umbrella from time to time and gave the present positions to the entire earth. The author proposed a major movement of Tectonic plates in the near past as it was needed to give present geological structure of the Earth. It is noteworthy that before 1405 BC, the North and South American continents were relatively close to the African continent.

If we think about the creator, he might be connected in this issue. Without this incident the entire African continent could be destroyed by Ice Age again in the near past. If 9.2 million square kilometres were green woodlands, green savannahs, then what had happened to the entire region, every time there were floods, floods and the population of entire region might have suffered a lot when compared to the small population that perished due to this mass devastation by heat.

It might be another region occupied and filled by Giant population as if in Atlantis at that time. These giants propagated the idea that Atlas was the god of the Universe and they initiated the theories about the end of the World by creating calendars just like the Mayans of Central America.

During formation of Sahara Desert the following multi-purpose acts occurred supernaturally:

1. To deluge Atlantis Island as the inhuman acts of giants crossed their limits on this land
2. To protect the entire African continent and region from ecological severe consequences
3. To stop the false religion spreading on earth propagated by Giants prevailed in that period
4. To give extra day light on the Arabian Tectonic Plate as an answer to Joshua's prayer in 1405 BC.

(This was explained in my book"Joshua's Long Day@ American Tectonic Plate Movements" which is available in Amazon.com)

The reader is advised to read the above book which explains the Tectonic Plate Movements and its effects on the face of the Earth. This book deals with the Joshua's Long day in 1405 BC and its link with American tectonic plate Movements. The present book deals with the formation of Sahara Desert in the near past and its link with Atlantis deluge in a single day and night in Atlantic Ocean. The author is excited to convey that because of the Tectonic Plate Movements and tilt of the Earth this great devastation occurred and the green land turned into the land of nothing in a flash.

CHAPTER FIVE

Earth's Tectonic Plates: Its Movements

Key Principles of Tectonic Plate Movements

The outer layers of the Earth are divided into lithosphere and asthenosphere. This is based on differences in mechanical properties and in the method for the transfer of heat. Mechanically, the lithosphere is cooler and more rigid, while the asthenosphere is warmer and flows more easily. In terms of heat transfer, the lithosphere loses heat by conduction, whereas the asthenosphere also transfers heat, but by convection and has a nearly adiabatic temperature gradient.

Due to heat transfer and convection currents of the lava inside the earth, the tectonic plates namely North and South American Plates started moving towards west and at the same time the land of Atlantis submerged under waters in single day and night and enormous amounts of sand with fire deposited on the North African lands forming high sand dunes in the region. The Green Sahara lands scorched and became a land of devastation in 1405 BC. At the same time, the African, Arabian plates and Eurasian plates stand still. So, the earth dwellers observed that Sun stood still and moon stayed there for about 23 hours and 20 minutes. At the same time, through the opened junctions of tectonic plates, huge amounts of sand and lava came out and poured upon the North African regions.

Sea Floor Spreading – subduction of the Plates

Graphic 07: Showing – sea floor spreading

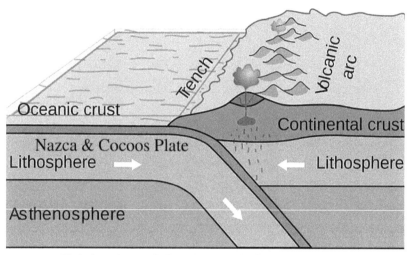

Subduction of the Nazca & Cocoos Plates
under American Plates

We have to understand the seafloor spreading of the oceanic crust before we can understand how the tectonic plates moved apart on Joshua's Long day. As the author mentioned, the North American and South American tectonic plates were close to the African continent before Joshua's Long Day. When Joshua ordered the Sun to stand still and moon in Ajalon, the two tectonic plates once started moving towards westward by the way of seafloor spreading in the mid-Atlantic Ocean. At the same time, the **Nazca and Cocos** plates were subducted into the mantle. As they belong to oceanic lithosphere, they went into the inner part of the earth and they melted. At the same time, the junctions of these plates wide open and huge amounts of sand with fire came out of the mantle just as projectile and deposited on North African region. These deposits remain as sand dunes spread across the North African region in a course of time after 1405 BC. This process started suddenly and the Tsunami from the Atlantic Ocean travelled towards west Africa deluging low-lying areas and the land of Atlantis deluged in a single day and terrible night in the day when the Sun stood still and moon stayed.

"Seafloor spreading is a process that occurs at mid-ocean ridges, where new oceanic crust is formed through volcanic activity and then gradually moves away from the ridge. Seafloor spreading helps explain continental drift in the theory of plate tectonics. When oceanic plates diverge, tensional stress causes fractures to occur in the lithosphere. Basaltic magma rises up the fractures and cools on the ocean floor to form new sea floor. Older rocks will be found farther away from the spreading zone while younger rocks will be found nearer to the spreading zone.

Earlier theories (e.g. by Alfred Wegener and Alexander du Toit) of continental drift were that continents 'ploughed' through the sea. The idea that the seafloor itself moves (and carries the continents with it) as it expands from a central axis was proposed by Harry Hess from Princeton University in the 1960s.[1] The theory is well accepted now, and the phenomenon is known to be caused by convection currents in the plastic, very weak upper mantle, or asthenosphere.

The new oceanic crust is quite hot relative to old oceanic crust, so the new oceanic basin is shallower than older oceanic basins. If the diameter of the earth remains relatively constant despite the production of new crust, a mechanism must exist by which crust is also destroyed. The destruction of oceanic crust occurs at subduction zones where oceanic crust is forced under either continental crust or oceanic crust. Today, the Atlantic basin is actively spreading at the Mid-Atlantic Ridge. Only a small portion of the oceanic crust produced in the Atlantic is subducted. However, the plates making up the Pacific Ocean are experiencing subduction along many of their boundaries which causes the volcanic activity in what has been termed the Ring of Fire of the Pacific Ocean. The Pacific is also home to one of the world's most active spreading centres (the East Pacific Rise) with spreading rates of up to 13 cm/yr. The Mid-Atlantic Ridge is a 'textbook' slow-spreading centre, while the East

Pacific Rise is used as an example of fast-spreading. The differences in spreading rates affect not only the geometries of the ridges, but also the geochemistry of the basalts that are produced.

Since the new oceanic basins are shallower than the old oceanic basins, the total capacity of the world's ocean basins decreases during times of active seafloor spreading. During the opening of the Atlantic Ocean, sea level was so high that a Western Interior Seaway formed across North America from the Gulf of Mexico to the Arctic Ocean."

Graphic-08: shows subduction and volcanic activity- seafloor spreading

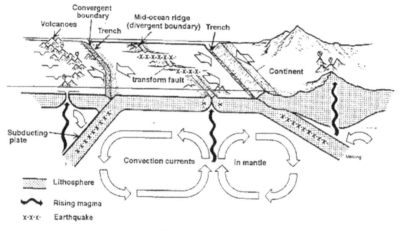

Figure 2. Sea-floor spreading. Modified from NSTA/FEMA (1988).

When North American Plate pulls apart, several things happen along the mid-Atlantic Ocean. Volcanic activity was severe there as the mantle easily moved to the surface and the land of Atlantis and the big constructions apparently mixed with lava flowed. As Atlantis is situated at the junction of tectonic plates, when the new ocean floor formed at the mid-Atlantic ridge, the North and South continents moved apart in day and a terrible night during Joshua's Long day. At the same time huge amounts of sand with fire and lava from inner earth came out as a great projectile and fell on the North African lands by scorching this area and submerging the green pastures, woodlands and green savannahs buried under great sand dunes. After terrible day due to the normal rotation of the earth the high sand dunes spread from west to east in the course of time. Many mountain ranges lost their greenery due to great heat and fire from the air. But this incident depicted as Sun scorched the land by the wrong driving of the Sun Chariot by Phaeton. The myth of Phaeton's story reveals the intensity of heat and devastation on North African lands.

The North American and South American Plates moved apart as divergent (spread away) tectonic plates. This divergent boundary formed of mountains in these junctions. The ridge at mid-Atlantic was spread with unusual speed by upwelling of magma from the mantle creating new ocean floor. So as the new ocean floor formed in the mid-Atlantic and the Plates moved apart in one single day and night. Ocean floor spreading occurred on large scale during Joshua's Long Day by magma is constantly streaming out to the surface, creating new ocean floor in the Atlantic Ocean. This magma was even travelled to the western lands of the Sahara forming a structure which will be explained in the next chapters.

At the same time the North and South American plates collided with Nazca and Cocos minor plates in the Pacific Ocean. These two oceanic lithosphere plates were subducted into the mantle along western coasts of these two continents, so that the earth's circumference was not changed. When these two plates subducted and melted in the mantle, the extra lava came out to form mountain range along the convergent boundaries. This happened along the western shores of North and South America. So even the North and South American plates moved thousands of kilometres in that terrible day and night there was no change in the circumference of the earth. The volume of the lava inside the earth is constant. Whenever subduction of plates took place, volcanic activity prevailed and the mountain ranges apparently formed along the convergent boundaries of the Tectonic plates. The author claims that the Andes and Rocky Mountains belong to this category.

Structure of the Earth.

(Quote: Henry David Thoreau wrote)

"The Lithosphere (outer layer) is divided into mobile plates. Plate tectonics describes the distribution and motion of the plates. The theory of plate tectonics grew out of earlier hypotheses and observations collected during explorations of the rocks of the ocean floor.

Graphic 09: picture showing earth and different layers

(This is also taken from Internet.)

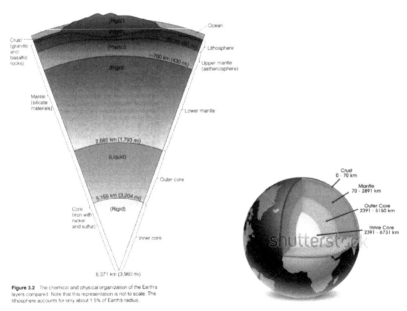

Layers of the Earth   Earth's interior structure

There are three major layers (crust, mantle, core) within the earth that are identified on the basis of their different compositions.

The uppermost mantle and crust can be subdivided vertically into two layers with contrasting mechanical (physical) properties. The outer layer, the Lithosphere, is composed of the crust and uppermost mantle and forms a rigid outer shell down to a depth of approximately melted rocks in the upper mantle that acts in a plastic manner on long-time scales. The asthenosphere extends from about 100 to 300 KM depth. The theory of plate tectonics proposes that the Lithosphere is divided into a series of plates that fit together like the pieces of a jigsaw puzzle."

Now we are dealing with the North and South American plate movements at an unusual speed on Joshua's long day and the Atlantis was deluged in the Atlantic Ocean. In order to understand these plate movements, we have to refer to sources such as geologists who provided valuable theories and lessons on this subject. The main objection may be which force caused to move these plates apart at high speed in single day and night. Here, geologists and scientists propose the convection currents in the mantle make this possible. This occurred because of an Act of God. As we believe that God is the creator of this universe, he can do what he intended to do, to fulfil his purposes. Some may argue that, how it was reasonable to drown a society which was flourishing in those days. But we should remember that they propagate false belief systems in those days about future. Mayan calendar was the main evidence and this belief system came from their mother civilization Atlantis. We have observed the news and how the people were terrified about the end of the world on 21 Dec, 2012. This was sample of the Atlantis belief system. God has his own reasons to do something on the earth. Here I should mention the same belief system was existed in case of giants may be on the North African region before 1405 BC. If this was the case, removing these giants from North African region is one of the purposes of devastating this region.

Graphic 10: Tectonic plate divisions mainly African, Eurasian, North & South American plates

Map showing Atlantis in Atlantic
Ocean with plate junctions.

From the above graphic we can observe that these tectonic plates namely African, Eurasian and North American Plates had junctions at a certain area that point is the actual location of Atlantis continent as described by Plato in the Pillars of Hercules.

The people of Atlantis did not know that their beautiful, wonderful continent was poorly situated at the junction of the four tectonic plates. After the global flood, around the time of Peleg (Genesis 10:25), the Earth got divided for the very first time. This island might have flourished after the flood and until the time of Joshua as per Biblical history. During that separation, it is possible that the Atlantis continent formed as the lava came out from the mantle of the earth at these junctions.

Peleg's grandfather was Salah and it means "send, scatter, make somebody to flee" might be that the scattering of the people happened when Salah was born. It was 37 years after the flood. They had actually 64 years to go to their ordered territories by God before the continental drift.

As Plato mentioned, the continent was navigable from the Pillars of Hercules, and the size of the continent taking into consideration the central part of Atlantis should be at the junction of three tectonic plates i.e., present Azores. It is learned that in the central area, the Giants lived and in outer rings the subjugated tribes around them. The geologists calculated the movement of tectonic plates is only few centimetres per year. This rate is true for today. But in the beginning, God said that in Genesis account as a part of third-day creation "and God said, let the waters under the heavens be gathered together into one place, and let the dry land appear". And it was so God called the dry land Earth, and the waters that were gathered he called Oceans.(Genesis 1: 8-10)

We should observe for this act it took only a part of a day to God to bring together all the Tectonic plates together. So, the tectonic plates gathered or diverged at different speeds as the case may be and this might be done by God and God alone no force in this universe can move these gigantic continental or oceanic plates moves at such high speeds. We should not compare earth's tectonic plates present speed to other incidents that occurred by God's intervention in ancient times. From the beginning, the plates might be moved at different speeds as it was possible with God.

It is clear that the North American plate and South American tectonic plates were at navigable distance and had their junction beneath the Atlantis continent. Geologists are at a thought of millions of years of time to spread the continents to present positions. But if we can observe carefully that much of time not necessary as I have explained earlier by taking Genesis account as example.

It was noteworthy that Geologists found that North American and South American plates are divergent towards west and African plates convergent towards north. So these two plates travelled towards west at certain speed with opposite speed to the rotational speed of the earth towards east. Here I should mention that African Plate and other plates of the earth stood still for 23 hours and 20 minutes and by miracle of God North & South American Plates travelled west causing terrible demise of Atlantis in one day and night. On the same day the opening up of Tectonic plates under Atlantis occurred and the sand and fire poured in a massive way just like a projectile towards North African region depositing vast amounts of sand and the lava particularly poured on a spot for some hours. The inner force is very extravagant and the lava from the junction of American tectonic plate came out with enormous force and travelled towards west and deposited on a spot in North African region. The lava deposited in this spot spread across the region making the area with some concentric rings of basaltic and sandstones. This spot became the wonder of the world in this modern society. The formation of this spot was certainly linked with Atlantis deluge. So much information is given about the tectonic plate movements which is essential to understand this book. The spot will be revealed in the next chapter.

CHAPTER SIX

Atlantis Deluge @ Joshua's Long Day

There were many assumptions and speculations about the existence and demise of Atlantis. We have to understand that Atlantis was not an Antediluvian world. During the global flood every human being including Nephilim on the earth was destroyed. As the author mentioned earlier, after global flood the descendants of Noah, after the attempt to build Tower of Babel, they were searching for new lands and continents to live. In the post-flood arena while going west ward from Babel travelling from place to place, after certain period they found a nice landscape or continent against the pillars of Hercules. At the time of reaching this land these people found this continent was navigable with small boats and ships from the land of Portugal, Europe. They might be travelled through the Mediterranean Seashore in those days. Anyhow, they reached this beautiful land flourishing with green pastures and different kinds of trees as it was a land formed by volcanic activity. This continent was formed due to the lava expelled from the junctions of North, South America Tectonic Plates, Africa and Eurasian tectonic plates.

This continent may be formed during creation period or during the global flood. This continent was full of Rocky Mountains and plenty of plants and glaciers. Here we must observe that this is a land **of hot and cold-water fountains**. So they inhabited the land and cultivated it, forming and cattle breeding were going on.

As Genesis account reveals to us that after the flood there were Nephilim existed (Genesis 6:4) on the face of the earth, we can understand that 1500 years after the global flood again Sons of God intermarried the women on this continent and again began a race of Nephilim. It is noteworthy that Atlas was a Nephilim.

God never tolerated the hybrid generation of fallen angels who intended to pollute humans. Whenever the fallen angels tried to pollute humans, which were created in the image of God, there should be a reaction evident from the heaven. Many people reject the salvation plan of God, which is up to them whether accepted to enter heaven or rejected to be perish. But when earth was in jeopardy because of the acts of some fallen ones there should be an action from above.

As a part of divine operation in removing the Nephilim from the earth and a time came to God took this decision of deluging this land. The pride, greediness and sun worship, animal sacrifices and false theories about future and framing calendars and assuming dates for end of the world, activities were viewed seriously as the source of these things were fallen angels. All these activities came to the notice of God almighty and decided to remove this other Babel from the face of the earth.

This occurred at the time of Joshua the God's warrior. Joshua 10: 11-13 reads: "And it came to pass, as they fled from before Israel, and were in the going down to Beth-heron, that the Lord cast down great stones from heaven upon them unto Azekah, and they died. Then spoke Joshua to the Lord in the day when the Lord delivered up the Amorites before the children of Israel, and he said in the sight of Israel, Sun, stand thou still upon Gibeon; and thou, Moon, in the valley of Ajalon. The Sun stood still, and the moon stayed, until the people had avenged themselves upon their enemies. Is not this written in the book of Jasher? So, the Sun stood still amid heaven, and hasted not to go down about a whole day".

It appears to have been midday or before the sunset, the Sun did not proceed to set for a period of completed day, which many commentators take to be approximately a 24-hour period, rather than just a day light period. Many cultures have records of legends that seem to be based on this event. For example, there is a Greek myth of Apollon's son, Phaethon which was clearly explained in this book who disrupted the Sun's course for a day. And since Joshua's 10th chapter is historical, cultures around the globe should have long days and nights evidently. We have long days in African continent and in New Zealand Māori people have a myth about how their hero Maui showed the sun before it rose, while the Mexican Annals of Cuauhtitlan records a night that continued for and extended for an extended time.

It should also be noted that the Amorites were sun and moon worshippers. For these 'gods' to have been forced to obey the God of the universe. This must have been a devastating experience for the Amorites, and this might well have been the reason why God performed this particular miracle at Joshua's time. The Israelis were almost at the point of occupation of the land of Canaan by the help of God.

What did Christian scholars say about the time of demise?

(Quote: got questions .org, "Does he Bible mention the lost city of Atlantis? Is there any evidence for Atlantis)

"The city of Atlantis was a mythological island nation first mentioned in Plato's writings around 360 BC. He claimed to have based his information on manuscript given to the Athenian Solon (638- 558 BC) by an Egyptian priest. Atlantis supposedly had conquered Italy and North Africa but was pushed back by Athens shortly thereafter; the island disappeared into the sea.

Plato speaks of Atlantis in the dialogues 'Timaeus and Critias'. In the text, Socrates ponders if a perfect society could ever exist, and Critias tells the story of Atlantis. According to Critias, Atlantis was about 230 miles long 340 miles wide and lay in the Atlantic Ocean, west of the Rock of Gibraltar. According to the mythology, Poseidon's sons, including Atlas, lived there. It was destroyed around 9600 BC by earthquakes and a flood. Plato's contemporaries were spilt as to whether Plato really believed Solon's account. The early Christian scholars Clement and Tertullian seemed to think Atlantis was real. There is a discussion today as to whether Solon mistranslated the date in the Egyptian hieroglyphics, counting hundreds as thousands; if Solon was in error, then Atlantis destruction was **closer to 1500 BC.**"

So here from the above quote we can understand the Solon's account of Atlantis demise is in error. Anyhow, the date proposed by the scholars was very near to the date of Joshua's long day i.e 1405 BC. Atlantis disappeared from the Atlantic Ocean, all in a single day. This fact links with the Joshua's long day. With God's help, the sun and moon stayed in the space for about one day. The Bible was written in terms of geocentric attitude because at that time all believed that Earth was the centre and all other heavenly bodies moving around it. But at this time of space exploration we have knowledge about the earth's rotation.

(Quote: Atlantis: The Mystery Unravelled, page 30, the desiccation and the great fire, Historical basis of The Atlantis Legend)

"The contemporary documents declare with certainty that such catastrophes did in fact occur towards the end of the 1300 BC (i.e., 1390 to 1410 BC Edgerton). One source says of the desiccation and the great fire: **'A terrible torch hurled flames from the sky to seek the souls of Libyans and to destroy their tribe.'** Edgerton explains that lightening from the sky had affected the Libyans and destroyed their tribe. Similar details may be found elsewhere. "The heat burned like a flame on their land. Their bones burned and melted in their limbs."

"The heat in their land burned like a fire in an oven"**. And, concerning the North people: "Their forests and people were destroyed by the fire." "Before they spread a sea of flames. Repeatedly we find it recorded that the enemies of Egypt were burned or afflicted by the great fire. But Egypt also suffered. An eyewitness has reported that walls, gales and columns were destroyed by flames, the sky was in chaos, no fruit or food could**

be found, in a single day everything was destroyed and the land was left to dry out lie cut flax".

Please observe the above phrase that a terrible torch hurled flames from the sky. This statement is evident that flames of fire and sand poured upon the North African lands and molten lava poured upon a spot in the western Africa.

On the same day, the fire and sand came out of the junctions in Atlantic Ocean and poured upon the North African lands on massive scale. At the beginning of opening up of the tectonic plates and huge amount of lava travelled just like a projectile from Atlantic Ocean and landed on a certain spot which formed a concentric circle of lava and sandstone deposits on circular form about 50 km diameter in this region. This structure remains as a spectacular view from the space and some are assuming it as Atlantis as it is circular in shape.

Graphic-11: Eye of the Sahara

(Photo credit: NASA / SPL / Barcroft Images / Barcroft Media via Getty Images)

From the above quote we can understand that Libya was affected badly and severely. Libya was near Atlantis and the fire raged from the tectonic plate junctions pushed out in the direction of Libya and Egypt. Unlike a Volcano, due to very high pressure inside the earth, it is like torch coming out with tremendous speed and that fire may reach even western Egypt in those days.

So we can come to conclusion that Joshua's long day was an historical fact and we will discuss how the Sun stood still and Moon in the land of Canaan. Thus, we assume the date of the disappearance of Atlantis one day and night must be on the day of Joshua's Long day which was occurred in 1405 BC. This matches with the destruction of Minoan and Crete cultures in the Mediterranean Sea. In this context, we must think about the Plato's story of Atlantis demise in one single day and night. This phrase gives much scope to research again about the facts of Atlantis. We know that the volcanic eruptions starts slowly and they lasts for months and even years. Here, as far as Atlantis was concerned, it disappeared on one unfortunate night. This point is the key of this book. Joshua asked the Lord to make the sun stand still for extra day light and the Atlantis was destroyed in one day and night. So, there was a link between Joshua's Long Day and the Demise of Atlantis by severe earthquakes and tidal waves. On the same day the lava with great pressure came out from the junctions of tectonic plates in Atlantic Ocean just like a projectile and poured upon a spot. The lava poured on that spot on a massive way formed a spectacular structure that is going to be revealed in this book. The moments of Tectonic Plates only through the convection currents of lava inside the earth and the author is assuming the tilt of the earth for these massive movements towards west. Let us discuss about the tilt of the earth and its consequences.

CHAPTER SEVEN
Tilt of the Earth

The Earth is one of the planets of the solar system. Our star, sun is part of the Milky Way galaxy. The Milky Way is a barred spiral galaxy that contains billions of stars including our Sun. The Earth orbits around the sun which is just one of the countless stars in the Milky Way galaxy.

We know that the universe is vast and contains billions or even trillions of galaxies each with their own stars, planets and celestial objects. The exact position of the Earth within the universe is constantly varying as everything is in motion with galaxies moving relative to one another.

It is imperative to note that the size of the Universe is immense and our understanding of its scale and structure is continuously evolving through scientific discoveries and space explorations. New galaxies are being discovered every year. After sending the James Webb telescope to the space the span of reaching outer space evidently increased and galaxies being found and some habitable planets were also found but they are all at a distance of hundreds of light years. One light year is equal to approximately 9.460 trillion kilometres. This reveals us how big our universe is.

Earth's Tilt and its affects

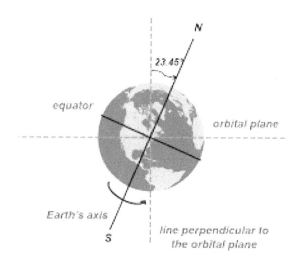

Graphic 12: Tilt of the Earth 23.5 degrees (This graphic also taken from the Internet.)

The tilt of the Earth refers to its axial tilt which is approximately 23.5 degrees east. This tilt plays a crucial role in determining the seasons and climate patterns on the planet. As the Earth orbits the Sun different parts of the Earth receive different amounts of sunlight throughout the year due to this tilt.

Consequences of the Earth's tilt:

1. <u>Seasonal variations</u>**:** The tilt of the Earth causes the angle at which sunlight reaches various parts of the planet to change throughout the year. These results in the four seasons namely spring, summer, autumn and winter. Areas tilted towards the sun experience summer while areas tilted away from the sun experience winter.

2. <u>Varying day length</u>: The tilt of the Earth affects the length of Daylight during different seasons. During summer, the hemisphere tilts towards the Sun in which case days are

longer. But during winter days are shorter. This variation in day length has an impact on agriculture, human activities and wildlife behaviour.

3. <u>Climate patterns</u>: The author believes that tilt of the Earth occurred in 1405 BC and this tilt towards east accelerated the speed of the North, South American Tectonic Plates in Atlantic Ocean and great devastation experienced by North African Lands. This tilt influenced global climate patterns in the prehistoric times. When the sand and fire came from the junctions of four tectonic plates namely North, South American Plates and African, Eurasian plates under the land of Atlantis, due to fire and sand from sky changed the fate of the region and because of the tilt the temperature change continued from 1405 BC.

The author believes that in 1405 BC on Joshua's Long day, the Earth tilted towards east 23.5 degrees and the North and South American Tectonic Plates travelled westward by the viscosity of the lithosphere. This was the mini-doomsday in the near past because the Earth tilted and the Tectonic Plates under Atlantis wide open and sand fire came out of inner Earth with enormous force. The tilt of the earth affected entire area as the lava from the junctions of tectonic plates in Atlantic Ocean deposited on a single spot to become a mysterious place even in this scientifically advanced society.

The tilt of the Earth stopped the humidity of because of greenery and green forests in this region. The green Sahara advocates higher humidity before 1405 BC and in turn the floods might have been common in North African region and entire African continent affected by heavy rains continuously. This situation may be unbearable for the humans in this region.

What would happen to the Earth if it was not tilted?

Earth not being tilted would have a profound impact on seasonal changes in temperature, sunlight and precipitation. It plays a vital role in the growth and development of the crops. If the Earth did not tilt, the entire planet, rather most importantly the North African region in great danger of floods and ecological imbalance.

Meteorologist Jeff Haby once said,

"At present, the Earth is tilted 23.5 degrees on its axis. This is the primary reason for the seasons. When the Earth is tilted toward the sun the Northern Hemisphere is in the warm season and when the Earth is tilted away from the Sun the Northern Hemisphere is in the cool season. Since the Earth revolves at a predictable and relatively steady rate around the sun the cycle repeats itself every year. In the warm season, the sun is higher in the sky and it is warmer and in the cool season the sun is lower in the sky and it is cooler.

In case the earth didn't tilt, the plane of the Earth's poles would always be perpendicular to the sun. The sun would always be just on the horizon 24 hours a day every day at the poles. Every day would be like what it currently is on the Equinox since every location on Earth would have about a 12-hour sunlight day and the noon sun angle would be about the same every day. There would no longer be season as we know them. The temperature and precipitation pattern would not change much. It would still be warm at the equator and cold at the poles. The most profound impact on temperatures would be at the poles. Instead, and dark and frigid temperatures in the winter and warmer and constant sun in the summer, the polar areas would have much more uniform temperatures year-round and the sun would always be low on the horizon. Across the Earth it would be like it is in the middle of fall or spring but it would last all year every year.

Would there be any differences at all?

Yes, there would still be some slight changes during the year even though there would not be seasons as we know them now. The Earth-Sun distance does vary during the year. Currently, the sun is closest to Earth in the Northern Hemisphere winter and further away in summer. With no tilt, this change in Earth-Sun distance during the year would produce a slight impact on the weather pattern. It must be emphasized the impact would be small since the Earth-Sun distance is not significantly different during the year (91.4 million miles in January compared to 94.5 million miles in July). Earth having tilt has a far greater impact on the weather pattern but without any tilt the Earth-Sun distance would have the dominant impact on season".

R K Naresh

Sardar Vallabhbhai Patel University of Agriculture and Technology

"More tilt means more severe seasons warmer summers and colder winters; less tilt means less severe seasons cooler summers and milder winters. It's the cool summers that are thought to allow snow and ice to last from year-to-year in high latitudes, eventually building up into massive ice sheets. The seasons are caused by the tilt of the earth's axis and revolution of the earth around the sun. If the earth's axis had not been tilted to the plane of its orbited then there would have been no seasons and humanity would have suffered. Earth spins at an angle of around 23.5-degrees; if that axial tilt were to change enough to spin sideways on its axis; whole portions of the planet could be plunged into darkness or thrown into direct sunlight for months at a time. If earth did not tilt and orbited in an upright position around the sun, there would be minor variations in temperatures and precipitation throughout each year as Earth moves slightly closer and farther away from the sun. In short, we would not have any seasons. This is why the Earth's 23.5 degree tilt is all important in changing our seasons. Near June 21st, the summer solstice, the Earth is tilted such that the Sun is positioned directly over the Tropic of Cancer at

23.5 degrees north latitude. This situates the northern hemisphere in a more direct path of the Sun's energy. The axis of rotation of the Earth is tilted at an angle of 23.5 degrees away from vertical, perpendicular to the plane of our planet's orbit around the sun. The tilt of the Earth's axis governs the warming strength of the sun's energy. The Earth's axis is tilted at an angle of 23.5 degrees. This means that the Northern Hemisphere gets more sunlight in the summer than the Southern Hemisphere, and vice versa in the winter. If the Earth's axis were not tilted, we would not have seasons".

The author proposed that the tilt of the Earth occurred on a single day. In order to maintain the ecological balance of earth, this tilt occurred by an Act of God. At the same time, lava came out with great force just like a projectile and deposited on a spot in the North African region as shown in the image on the previous pages. After this incident, sand and fire came out of the junctions of these plates followed and deposited in the western African region. The rotation of the earth resumed as usual after this particular day of devastation in 1405 BC.

What would happen if the Earth stopped rotating for a day?

If the rotation of the Earth was to suddenly stop for 24 hours, the consequences would be terrible and significant. Firstly, the most noticeable effect would be the loss of the apparent motion of the sun across the sky. This occurred on Joshua's Long Day in the pre-historic period.

In 1405BC when Joshua's Long Day occurred in the Middle East, the noticeable effect was the Sun stood still in the sky as mentioned in the book of Joshua 10:12. The Arabian and African Tectonic Plates stood still and North, South American Tectonic Plates travel westward with unusual speed. On the same day from the junctions of these plates in Atlantic Ocean huge amounts of sand, lava and fire came out from the outer mantle of the Earth, devastating the North African lands in a single day and night. The Atlantis was deluged in the Atlantic Ocean by merging into the sea floor spreading taken place in Atlantic Ocean. The mud in the Atlantic Ocean was another clue that sea floor spreading activated in the near past. So the Atlantis ruins mixed with lava and covered by mud evolved from the junctions on that particular day. This was massive and it was not possible to remove mud and excavate the Atlantis in the middle of the Atlantic Ocean. We know that volcano erupted on earth the fertile soil will deposit on the earth, but in Atlantic Ocean this erupted soil became mud. Please note this point.

The Sun had appeared to stop moving and remain fixed in one position for about 24 hours on the land of Israel. The other consequences happened with drastic changes in the Earth's atmosphere and weather patterns mainly on the North African lands. On the same day, the Mega Tsunami proceeded from the Atlantic Ocean devastating the North Africa and followed by huge amounts of sand and fire poured on Mauritania and Mali where we can observe sand dunes in different positions. These sand dunes were deposited as an outburst of sand and fire from the junctions of North, South American and African, Eurasian Tectonic plates under Atlantis. Before 1405 BC, Atlantis mentioned by Plato was relatively close to African continent and junctions also close to the north African Lands (as shown the graphics in the previous chapters). The lava proceeded from the junction was deposited on a certain spot and the liquid lava spread across the area by creating a structure which is a wonder to the modern society and it was detected by astronauts from the space.

The cessation of Earth's rotation for about 24 hours had significant and potentially catastrophic consequences mentioned above in the North African lands. It is important to note that there had no historical records about this geological change as it took place in pre-historic timeline in 1405 BC.

The change in Earth's rotation in 1405 BC had long-term effects on Earth i.e., formation of Sahara Desert which regulates the atmosphere of the African continent in different seasons. If it not had happened, the entire region become green and the region stormed with continuous rains and floods. It was not good for the ecological balance of the Earth. So the tilt of Earth was allowed supernaturally and brought drastic changes in the ecological balance of the region and the Earth. Some decisions seem to be very inconvenient to some parts of the people but there might have been long run benefits to the planet. For some people, it was nature's act and for some it was divine act. It depends on their perception and belief system. But the fact is the human mind cannot perceive the acts upon the earth if they occurred in a massive way. This is the case regarding Eye of the Sahara.

CHAPTER EIGHT
Green Sahara

(The following article is taken from the book 'When the Sahara was Green? by Martin Williams')

"The popular view of the Sahara is one of endless rolling sand dunes alternating with vast sand plains form which emerge occasional rocky hills. Nothing could be further from the truth. Only about a fifth of the Sahara actually consists of desert dunes and sand plains. The remaining four-fifths consists of rugged mountain ranges, vast sandstone or limestone plateaus and extensive gravel plains made up of fine wind-blown and alluvial sediments capped with a thin surface layer of fine gravel and stones. The word Sahara comes from the Arabic word "Sahra" meaning a wilderness or desolate land to be traversed as quickly as possible. One that certainly did not invite one to linger there.

One of the most striking aspects of the Sahara landscape is the abrupt change from steep hill slopes to very gentle foot slopes, which is quite unlike the landscape of rolling hills we know so well from Europe, North America and Asia with their deep soils and continuous cover of trees and grasses."

The author Martin Williams revealed us that the hills of Sahara Desert are quite different from the hills in other continents. So, the conclusion is that the Sahara Desert formed on flash and the sand fire devastated the hills in the region without having trees on the top of the hills. The terrible Tsunami filled the lower beds with salt water and we can find salt lakes in the midst of the Sahara. The geologists marvelled at the present situation of the hills because trees and vegetation are very rare on the top of the hills. The fire and sand completely changed the fate of the land and turned this region as a land of nothing.

The Sahara Desert used to be a Green Savannah and New Research Explains Why

A Landsat 8 photo of snow in the Sahara Desert, near the Algerian town of Ain Sefra.

Photo: NASA

Algeria's TassiliN'Ajjer plateau is Africa's largest national park. Among its vast sandstone formations, is perhaps the world's largest art museum. Over 15,000 etchings and paintings are exhibited there, some as much as 11,000 years old according to scientific dating techniques, representing a unique ethnological and climatological record of the region.

Curiously, however, these images do not depict the arid, barren landscape that is present in the TassiliN'Ajjer today. Instead, they portray a vibrant savannah inhabited by elephants, giraffes, rhinos and hippos. This rock art is an important record of the past environmental conditions that prevailed in the Sahara, the world's largest hot desert.

These images depict a period approximately 6,000-11,000 years ago called the Green Sahara or North African Humid Period. There is widespread climatological evidence that during this period the Sahara supported wooded savannah ecosystems and numerous rivers and lakes in what are now Libya, Niger, Chad and Mali.

This greening of the Sahara didn't happen once. Using marine and lake sediments, scientists have identified over 230 of these greenings occurring about 21,000 years over the past eight million years. These greening events provided vegetated corridors which influenced species' distribution and evolution, including the out- of-Africa migrations of ancient humans.

These dramatic greenings would have required a large-scale reorganisation of the atmospheric system to bring rain to this hyper-arid region. But most climate models haven't been able to simulate how dramatic these events were.

As a team of climate modellers and anthropologists, we have overcome this obstacle. We developed a climate model that more accurately simulates atmospheric circulation over the Sahara and the impacts of vegetation on rainfall.

We identified why North Africa greened approximately 21,000 years over the past eight million years. It was caused by changes in the Earth's orbit precession – the slight wobbling of the planet while rotating. This moves the Northern Hemisphere closer to the sun during the summer months.

This caused warmer summers in the Northern Hemisphere, and warmer air is able to hold more moisture. This intensified the strength of the West African Monsoon system and shifted the African rain belt northwards. This increased Saharan rainfall, resulting the spread of savannah and wooded grassland across the desert from the tropics to the Mediterranean, providing a vast habitat for plants and animals.

Our results demonstrate the sensitivity of the Sahara Desert to changes in past climate. They explain how this sensitivity affects rainfall across North Africa. This is important for understanding the implications of present-day climate change (driven by human activities). Warmer temperatures in the future may also enhance monsoon strength, with both local and global impacts.

The author of this book agrees with the ideas of above article and further confirms that wobbling of the Earth and Tilt of the Earth took place in 1405 BC. The African Humid Period ended in the year of 1405 BC.

Earth's Changing Orbit

The fact that the wetter periods in North Africa have recurred every 21,000 years or so is a big clue about what causes them: variations in Earth's orbit. Due to gravitational influences from the moon and other planets in our solar system, the orbit of the Earth around the sun is not constant. It has cyclic variations on multi-thousand- year timescales. These orbital cycles termed Milankovitch cycles; they influence the amount of energy the Earth receives from the sun.

On 100,000- year cycles, the shape of Earth's orbit (or eccentricity) shifts between circular and oval, and on 41,000-year cycles the tilt of Earth's axis varies (termed obliquity). Eccentricity and obliquity cycles are responsible for driving the ice ages of the past 2.4 million years.

The third Milankovitch cycle is precession. This concerns Earth's wobble on its axis, which varies on a 21,000-year timescale. The similarity between the precession cycle and the timing of the humid periods indicates the precession is their dominant driver. Precession influences seasonal contrasts, increasing them in one hemisphere and reducing them in another. During warmer Northern Hemisphere summers, a consequent increase in North African summer rainfall would have initiated a humid phase, returning in the spread of vegetation across the region.

Green Sahara: African Humid Periods Paced by Earth's Orbital Changes

(By: Peter deMenocal and Jessica E. Tierney Copy write 2012 Nature Education)

Green Sahara: African humid periods paced by Earth's Orbital Changes Paleoclimate and archaeological evidence tells us that, 11,000-5,000 years ago, the Earth's slow orbital 'wobble' transformed today's Sahara Desert to a land covered with vegetation and lakes. As he crossed by caravan from Tripoli to Timbuktu in the mid-1800s, the German explorer Heinrich Barth became the first European to discover the then-mysterious prehistoric Saharan rock paintings and engravings, which we now know date back to the African humid Period, a humid phase across North Africa which peaked between 9,000and 6,000 years ago.

These masterfully-rendered images depict pastoral scenes with abundant elephants, giraffe, hippos, aurochs, and antelope, occasionally being pursued by bands of hunters. The Sahara is very likely the world's largest art museum with hundreds of thousands of elaborate engravings and paintings adoring rocky caves and outcrops. The incongruence of this lively image in such lifeless settings intrigued Barth, who noted that the art work "bears testimony to a state of life very different from that which we are accustomed to see now in these regions."

Graphic 13: Rock Art of the Sahara Desert.

Orbital Forcing of subtropical climate

The Earth's axial rotation is perturbed by gravitational interactions with the moon and the more massive planets that together induce periodic changes in the Earth's orbit, including a 100,000-year cycle in the shape of the orbit (eccentricity), a 41,000-year cycle in the tilt of Earth's axis (obliquity) and a 20,000 -year cycle in the "wobble" – many lie in the wobbles- of the Earth's axis (precession). All three of orbital cycles- called Milankovitch cycles- impact African climate on long geologic timescales, but the cycle with the most influence on the rains in Africa is the 'wobble' cycle, precession. The main climatic effect of precession is to shift the season when the Earth has its closest pass to the sun (perihelion)- the so-called precession of the equinoxes. Today, perihelion occurs in northern hemisphere winter but 10,000 years ago (half a precession cycle) it occurred in northern hemisphere summer, and summer radiation over North Africa was about 7% higher than it is today".

As mentioned in the above research paper the orbital change might be one of the reasons. But the author of this book believes that tilt of the Earth took place in a day of 1405 BC and the North, South American Tectonic plates travelled westward in a single day and night. A terrible nightmare occurred on the North African lands by Mega Tsunami wave from Atlantic Ocean came over to the North African lands and some of the big fishes rolled into this land by this great wave of Tsunami. It is noteworthy that from the junctions of Tectonic Plates lava poured out just like a projectile into a certain spot on Mauritania as it was in liquid stage the lava spread across the region in concentric circles in 1405 BC. This was done on massive scale that's why the humans wandering in this place could not recognise it as a circular structure. It is imperative to know that on this spot no evidence of volcanic activity but the rocks were belongs to the volcanic activity. So, it was a mystery and we will find a solution to this problem in the next chapters.

CHAPTER NINE
EYE of the Sahara

The Eye of the Sahara, also known as the Richat Structure, is a geological formation located in the Sahara Desert in Mauritania. It is a circular feature, intriguing and visually striking natural wonder.

Mystery of the EYE:

As the author explained in the previous chapters, the formation of Eye shaped crater in Mauritania is the lava projected from the four junctions of North, South American tectonic Plates and African and Eurasian Plates. Most probably from a point in the junctions with high pressure the lava came out of the mantle and deposited on a spot in Mauritania before actual movements of the North, South Tectonic plates towards west in a single day. Before 1405 BC the North and South American tectonic plates were relatively close to African continent. The mysterious Atlantis Island was also at a reachable distance in the Atlantic Ocean before 1405 BC. During the deluge of Atlantis in Atlantic Ocean the junctions of Tectonic plates wide open giving scope to the lava to travel towards west, just like a projectile at that time. The outer mantle pressure is very high as per the geologist records.

Graphic-14: The lava poured upon a spot in Mauritania

Alimodhin M.Sc in Geophysics & gold Medallist Osmania University gave clear idea about Units of pressure.

The SI units of pressure are Pascal 1Pa=1N meter square (one Newton of force on 1 sq.mt area is 1 Pa)

The outer mantle of the Earth experiences significant pressure due to the weight of the overlying layers. The pressure increases with depth as a result of the gravitational pull exerted by the mass of the Earth. Near the surface, the pressure is relatively low, but as we go deeper into the Earth, the pressure progressively increases. At the boundary between the upper and lower mantle, known as the transition zone, the pressure can reach several Giga Pascal's (G Pa). The outer mantle pressure is estimated above 80 giga Pascals. 1 G Pa =100,00,00,000 Newton/ Sq. Meters. These immense pressures play crucial roles in shaping the Earth's interior and influencing processes such as Tectonic Plate Movements and convection currents of the mantle.

When the junctions under Atlantis Island wide open the lava from the mantle came out with very high pressure, it poured upon a spot in Mauritania in 1405 BC forming the Eye of the Sahara. A terrible tsunami devastated from Atlantic Ocean and the North African lands filled with salt water. At the same time along the Atlantic ridge the sand and fire followed from the Atlantic Ocean upon the North African lands devastating the region on massive way. The geologists found water flow from the Eye of the Sahara towards low laying areas of the North African lands. The author believes that this happened in such massive way that it is difficult to human mind to perceives it.

Some are assuming that the Eye of the Sahara is the Atlantis. If it was so, where are the constructions and the canals of the Atlantis? The Eye of the Sahara was formed at a diameter of about 40-55 KMs. As per Plato's narrative the Atlantis was great city having canals in which the ships of that time pass through them. So, this site not fit to be the lost civilization Atlantis. According to geologists the Eye of the Sahara was formed by the molten sandstones, igneous and sedimentary rocks. There was no volcanic activity found at this spot but sandstone appeared in these rings. Further there was no evidence of asteroid collision at this spot because there was no depression formed at the Centre. The formation reveals that massive hot lava poured upon this spot creating this mysterious Eye of the Sahara.

But there was no volcanic activity found in this place. The author believes that the hot lava and sand with fire came out of the mantle with very great pressure (about 80 giga pascals) and just like ICBM (Inter Continental Ballistic Missile), it travelled and poured at a spot in Mauritania forming the present discovered Eye of the Sahara.

Richat Structure by Marie Look March 15, 2024 (Internet-based article)(By the same heading we can come across this article in Internet)

In the Western Sahara Desert lies a natural wonder that has intrigued scientists and adventurers for centuries. Known as the Richat structure or, more commonly, the Eye of the Sahara- this massive geological formation resembles as giant eye.

Consisting of a series of rings on the Adrar plateau, a prominent feature in northern Mauritania, the structure measures about 50 KM in diameter, making it highly visible even high above Earth. In the local dialect of Arabic, the people refer to it as "Guelb er Richat" meaning "the Eye of the Richat".

What created the Eye of the Sahara?

At first glance, the Richat Structure resembles a giant bull's eye, with its concentric rings and circular ridges. The distinctive circular shape sparked various early theories about its formation; with the theory even being that it was the site of the lost city of Atlantis.

Although some experts initially thought the Eye of the Sahara to be an enormous impact crater, subsequent studies proved the geologic curiosity had a more complex origin involving terrestrial processes. Thanks to modern geological research, including satellite imagery provided by organizations like the NASA Earth Observatory, scientists now know it to be an uplifted geological dome characterised by layers of sedimentary rocks that have been exposed over millions of years by wind and water erosion.

However the author of this book confirms that the Eye of the Sahara formed in recent past which is 1405 BC. Why 1405 BC? Is explained in this book clearly and open to the investigation and debate based on the issues mentioned in this book.

Composition of the Eye of the Sahara

The formation's concentric rings are primarily composed of sedimentary rocks, including sandstone and limestone. The outer rings of the structure are composed of harder, more resistant rock layers, while the innermost depressions consist of softer rock layers that have eroded more rapidly over time.

The sedimentary layers offer a glimpse into the Earth's past, recording millions of years of geological history. As hard as it may be to imagine in the Sahara Desert, the circular ridges of the Richat Structure have helped scientists study both wet and dry periods in the area's history.

The Eye of Sahara features an underlying alkaline igneous complex, including igneous rocks called gabbroic rocks, which form because of magmatic activity and hydrothermal alteration.

That's a fancy way of saying that the Earth's material became so hot it turned into magma, or liquid rock, and then forced itself into the surrounding rocks, slowly cooling into a crystalline structure.

(Yes, the author agrees with above comment Earth itself cannot do it itself and form the Eye of the Sahara. There was an acceptable reason for this geological event and it was discussed clearly in this chapter)

Erosion, both by wind and water, has all helped to sculpt the Richat Structure into its present form, exposing different rock types and creating its concentric layers and circular shape. Differential erosion rates between the softer and more resistant layers have further contributed to the striking appearance of the formation of the Eye.

Scientific significance of the Eye of the Sahara

One of the most fascinating aspects of the Richat Structure is its resemblance to an enormous Eye when you view it from space. This unique feature has captured the attention of scientists and astronauts alike. The Gemini astronauts captured images on the Gemini TV mission, and astronauts on the International Space Station have photographed the Eye of the Sahara too.

The Richat Structure's geological significance extends beyond its visual appeal. It provides valuable insights into Earth's geological processes, including the effects of tectonic forces, erosion and magmatic activity. Additionally, the presence of sedimentary layers has yielded evidences of past environments and possibly even early human activity.

Some researchers speculate that the Richat structure may have been inhabited by early hominids such as Homo erectus or homo heidelbergensis. They have found evidence of stone tool manufactory, including Acheulean tools (such as hand axes), in the surrounding landscape, suggesting that early people might have used this area of the Sahara Desert for short-term hunting or habitation.

The Heritage Daily explains the 'rhyolite rocks' have been interpreted as lava floods that are part of two distinct eruptive centres formed from the remains of two maars, a low- relief volcanic crater caused by phreatomagmatic eruption(an explosion came when groundwater comes into contact to lava or magma).

Rhyolite Rocks: These are a type of volcanic rock that are rich in silica and have a high viscosity. They typically have a light colour and can be found in various volcanic regions around the world. Rhyolitic rocks are known for their explosive eruptions due to the high gas content trapped within the viscous magma. They offer form domes, obsidian and pumice deposits. These rocks provide valuable insights into the volcanic activity and geological history of a region.

The above information clearly reveals that there was a volcanic activity at the Eye of the Sahara. But interestingly there were no volcanoes erupted in this place. Even if it was so, the flat concentric circle formation is unexplainable. Hence the author suggests that the lava and hot sand poured at this spot from the junctions of Tectonic Plates in the Atlantic Ocean. When a liquid molten material from the mantle of the Earth poured upon this spot, then this type of formation is evident. It was formed at a diameter of about 50 KMs and the human eye from the ground can't perceive this formation as a whole for many years. So, we can assume that some Nomads occupy this area in pre-historic period i.e after 1405 BC.

The author proposes that these eruptions came from the mantle of the Earth through a leak in the junctions with high pressure of the interior Earth it was travelled just like a projectile and has a high silica content which makes it highly viscosity and sticky. The author concludes that because of the high viscosity and huge massive out poured of lava made this phenomena and the Tsunami followed by this incident made all other water flowing impressions around the Eye of the Sahara.

The most Amazing Deserts in Africa by Regina Baily:

"Geologists have concluded that the Eye of the Sahara is a geologic dome. The formation contains rocks that are at least 100 million years old; some date back to well before the appearance of life on the Earth. These rocks include igneous (volcanic) deposits as well as sedimentary layers that form as the wind pushes layers types of igneous rock in the area of the eye, including Kimberlitic, carbonatites, black basalts (similar to what can be seen in the big island of Hawaii) and rhyolites.

Millions of years ago, volcanic activity from deep beneath Earth's surface lifted the entire landscape around the Eye. These regions were not deserts, as they are today. Instead, they were likely much more temperate, with abundant flowing water. Layered sandstone rocks were deposited by blowing winds and on the bottoms of lakes and rivers during the temperate. The subsurface volcanic flow eventually pushed up the overlying layers of sandstone and other rocks. After the volcanism died down, wind and water erosion began to eat away at the domed layers of rock. The region began to settle down and collapse in on itself, creating thoroughly circular 'Eye feature.'

Many thanks to all researchers, geologists who spent their lifetime investigating the secret of Sahara Desert and Eye of the Sahara basing on the data and research outcomes available to them. In the above-mentioned work, there was a mention of volcanic activity because of the rocks present on the site. But the author of this book gives a solution for this problem. The lava and sand with fire came out of mantle under Atlantis which was situated at the four junctions of Tectonic Plates; lava came out of the Earth and pushed into the space just like a projectile poured on a spot in western Africa. Because of the viscosity and fire the concentric circle deposits formed at the spot, just like a hot liquid poured on a solid ground this type of formation will happen (up and down circular formation).

In 1405 BC, When the North, South American Tectonic Plates wide open due to the very high pressure of the mantle the volcanic substance travelled a long distance just like an arrow thrown into the air reached the western Africa.

Many mentioning the time of the rocks as millions of years old. Thanks to the modern dating process, this data is true as these deposits were inside the Earth for millions of years as the Earth existed for billions of years in this universe. The Scientists dating the rocks on the earth but they deposited them on the Earth in the near past i.e., 1405 BC. The carbon elements on Earth were exposed to severe heat on 1405 BC and the dating of the carbon deposits collected from Sahara might have mixed with the matter that came from inside the Earth. The sand with fire came from the mantle of the Earth and that sand scorched the greenery and woodlands on this region. So, the carbon dating of these particles may lead to a wrong conclusion. There should be a review of carbon dating the materials which are exposed to severe heat on that day. The author agrees that life of the rocks, dates back to millions of years and they were so. But not on the Earth surface, these materials were from inside the Earth.

The Time of the rocks on Earth is different from the date of igneous rocks from the mantle. We cannot compare the fossils on the Earth and the rocks came out of mantle and formed as a structure. We will discuss this item under the chapter Carbon dating.

In the above research wind and water erosion mentioned. Hence the author agrees with the water erosion. Initially it was started when the tectonic plates began to move and the rotation of the Earth partially stopped on Joshua's Long Day i.e., in 1405 BC. On this day a terrible Tsunami started and hit the West African shore when the Tectonic Plates began to move in Atlantic Ocean. This Mega Tsunami devastated the North African lands by depositing salt water in the laying areas and depressions and even in the Eye of the Sahara. This occurrence was very massive and about 50 km in diameter impression formed in the Mauritania which was a mystery even in this scientific world.

The salt deposits and shark and other marine fossils were evident as the Mega Tsunami immersed the North African lands. This type of Tsunami not been happened in the historic world of the Earth. In order to safely guard the climatic conditions of the Earth, the supernatural decision taken place to stop the rotation of the Earth partially, tilt of the Earth and North, South American Tectonic Plates travelled westward and African, Arabian Plates stood still on Joshua's Long Day which was recorded in Joshua10:12 of the Bible. If you agree with or not but it is true and a hidden mystery for centuries. The author requests all geologists to verify this claim not declining the hypothesis of the author.

Why a race removed from the Atlantis? The race that evolved in the land of Atlantis may propagate false belief systems on Atlantis and on nearby lands such as North African region they occupied. About this race the author gave more information about why the Atlantis was deluged in a single day and night in his previous title "Joshua's Long Day @ American Tectonic Plate Movements" which is available in Amazon.com

IFLSCIENCE Weekly Newsletter published an article:

The Eye of the Sahara is A Geological Mystery "staring Into Space" by Charlie Haigh, writes:

"When viewed from above, the eye of the Sahara looks just like an enormous impact crater sitting in the middle of the Sahara Desert of Mauritania. Stretching about 50 KM in diameter, comprised of a series of uniform ripples, this crater-sequel anomaly is in fact entirely terrestrial.

This spectacular ancient ecological formation was used in the 1960s by Gemini astronauts as a landmark. Geologists initially believed the Eye of the Sahara, as the Richat Structure, to be an enormous impact crater. However, further studies into the sedimentary rock making up the central dome have dated the formation back up the central dome have dated the formation back to the late Proterozoic, between 1 billion and 542 million years ago."

The above article mentioned the Eye of the Sahara was terrestrial and also formed billions of years ago. But the author did not agree with the time mentioned above. This formation belonged to pre-historic period and it has a link with Joshua's Long Day in biblical history.

It is noteworthy that some still believe the Structure is actually the remains of the lost City of Atlantis, as its circular shape is said to resemble the land described by Plato, but we are not entering that here....

Journal of African Earth Sciences: The researchers proposed an entirely different formation and explanation of the Eye. The presence of volcanic rock is said to suggest evidence of molten rock being pushed to the surfaces, causing the dome shape, before being eroded into the rings we see today. The paper proposed the separation of the supercontinent Pangaea may have played a part in these volcanic formations and tectonic shifts.

The structure is made up of a mixture of sedimentary and igneous rock. Erosion across the structure's surface reveals fine- grained rhyolite and course crystalline gabbro rocks that have undergone hydrothermal alteration. The types of rock formed across the rings erode at different speeds, creating different coloured patterns across the surface. Large sharp-angled fragments of sedimentary rock called mega breccia add to the swirling colourful irregularities that make up the formation.

The dome centre contains a limestone dolomite shelf with kilometre-wide breccia, ring dikes and alkaline volcanic arc. The complex geological structure of the Eye has puzzled and interested geologists since its discovery, and it is still widely considered to be one of the most impressive geological features in the world. As such, in 2022 it became one of the first 100 geological heritage sites recognised by the International Union of Geological Science (IUGS).

Due to its vast size, the Eye of the Sahara is best viewed from great heights (preferably space), so far now we'll have to rely on satellite images to bask in all its glory".

The above article gives us clear idea about the Eye of the Sahara and the structure contains alkaline volcanic rocks. Volcanic rocks without volcanic activity in the spot not possible in any way. But here is the mystery that the lava from the mantle through a hole in the Tectonic Plates in North Atlantic Ocean made possible this structure while two plates namely North, South American plates travel westward in a single day and night. On the same day and night the ancient city deluged into the depths of Atlantic Ocean merging in the lava came out from the mantle. On the same occasion the Arabian and African Plates stood still for a day supporting the phenomena of Sun stood still in the space and moon in the sky. At the same time lava from the mantle comes out with 100s of G Pa (Giga Pascals) pressure poured upon a spot on the west African lands forming a structure on this spot which is Eye of the Sahara and its rings.

The assumption of Atlantis in this spot is not suitable because Plato mentioned Atlantis as a big island of size of Asia Minor and Libya together and also, he narrated the Atlantis in Atlantic Ocean against the Pillars of Hercules. The 50 KMs diameter structure of the Eye of the Sahara is not fit to the above assumption of Atlantis. The Atlantis deluged in Atlantic Ocean and much volcanic activity occurred along the Atlantic ridge in the Atlantic Ocean.

Further evidence of millions of tons of mud accumulated in the Atlantic Ocean is another evidence of volcanic activity in the Atlantic Ocean and it is not possible to remove the mud to get archaeological evidence of Atlantis merged ruins in Atlantic Ocean.

The lava out of mantle travelled and poured with great pressure and reached the western parts of the North African lands and terrible Tsunami hit this region which was not experienced in the historic period of the Earth. It was happened in 1405 BC. Why 1405 BC? It was the year of Joshua's Long Day in the Biblical history. The author is confident to confirm this year as the doomsday of pre-historic times and led to many atmospheric changes taken place around the globe and the African continent was saved from green Sahara formation which would have impacted badly the entire region with continuous floods and devastation in the history of mankind.

An article from 'Geographical' by Grace Gourlay (21 Feb 2024)

"From the air, it appears as a vast bull's eye in the middle of the Sahara Desert. The symmetrical geological marvel in the Adrar plateau, a rocky, located region in Mauritania, it is known as the Eye of the Sahara or more recently, the Richat Structure.

Initially believed to be an impact structure resulting from a meteor, subsequent studies established it true nature as an uplifted geologic dome. It is 40 km in diameter and exposes concentric rings of rock created by erosion with a center dome nearly 20 KMs wide.

The force of erosion has sculpted this structure, forming distributive circular ridges known as cuestas and creating a remarkable circular pattern with sedimentary and igneous rocks. The rings have different rocks of various ages, and the ridges are mostly made of Quartzite.

While locals have known about it for millennia, it is hard to comprehend fully from the ground level. It was the first astronauts who drew scientific attention to the structure, assuming it was a meteor crater.

On-the-ground research discovered that it was, in fact, formed by erosion over millions of years. The erosion has exposed spectacular scatterings of rhyolites and gabbro- igneous rocks deep beneath the Earth's surface.

Beyond its geological wonders, the Richat Structure holds archaeological significance. Excavations have uncovered evidence of human activity, including Acheulean and pre-Acheulian artefacts. Acheulean tools, associated with Homo erectus and homo heidelbergensis (from around 2 million years ago), reveal a history of tool factoring and hunting activities.

The distribution of Acheulean tools serves as a historical record influenced by paleo-climatic factors. The Sahara's fluctuating climate, played a role in shaping the lifestyles of early inhabitants, fostering a hunter-gather way of life.

Despite the scientific exploration explaining the geological and archaeological narrative of the Richat Structure, some still claim the Eye of Sahara is evidence of the lost city of Atlantis. They claim it corresponds with Plato's depictions of Atlantis".

In the above article the writer mentioned a rock 'Quartzite' which means a metamorphic rock that is formed from sandstone under high heat and pressure. So, the author of this book believes that the lava and sand with fire came out of the mantle which experienced high pressure and came out of the junctions of four tectonic plates namely North, South American Plates and African and Eurasian Plates. It was a marvel to our comprehension and it was a reality. After pouring out of lava on this spot followed by great Tsunami overflowing the North African lands including Richat Structure in 1405 BC.

The Atlantis was situated at the four junctions of Tectonic Plates in Atlantic Ocean and in 1405 BC when Joshua prayed for extra day light in Israel, the North, South American Tectonic Plates travelled westward in an unusual speed deluging the Atlantis in Atlantic Ocean in one night. On the same day, the lava came out with great pressure and poured upon a spot in Mauritania in West Africa, a terrible Tsunami from Atlantic Ocean followed this incident as the North, South Tectonic Plates wide open due to the higher pressure of the mantle fire and sand poured upon the North African lands. The salt deposits were found everywhere in the Sahara was the reason because of this Tsunami. It might be the case once the entire Atlantic Ocean rampaged into the North African Lands by western coast or through Mediterranean Sea. This land is full of marine fossils and the species belonged to the salt seas. This terrible Tsunami was deposited all these marine species into this land by water flowing into these lands in a massive way. As the author mentioned earlier it was a semi-doomsday and many geological occurrences taken place in a massive way turning the North African lands as a place of nothing. The spot where the lava in liquid state just like a projectile poured upon the a spot due to high pressure in the mantle and deposited on this spot on Mauritania resulting formation of a spectacular structure which was called later as Richat Structure and **Eye of the Sahara**. The sand deposited on the western African spread the sand dunes into new lands as the Sahara expanding today.

CHAPTER TEN
Why this devastation?

The devastation is terrible and we have to think about the reasons for catastrophe in the near past. If North African lands continue to have high humidity as it was before 1405 BC, the geologists and climatologists suggest a climatic pattern of continuous rains and floods everywhere in this region and other parts of the earth affected in a negative way. So high humidity in Africa, such a high land mass attracts monsoons every time and there was continuous flooding of the region and there was a danger of went this region into ice age again.

If the entire Sahara Desert were to become green it would have a significant impact on the ecological balance of this land. It would also disrupt regional weather patterns and ecosystems.

In case there were no hot waves and arid conditions in North Africa entire region may be in jeopardized. So the supernatural intervention needed in this region as Joshua prayed for extra day light on that day of 1405 BC. The miracle of Sun stood still in the sky happened as the African and Arabian Tectonic Plates stood for about 24 hours. The same day the North, South American Tectonic plates travelled westward causing terrible Tsunami in Atlantic Ocean and this devastation in this land. It is a fantasy to all how these massive plates travel with high speed in a single day and night. But it is true and the devastation is evident on North African lands when the rotation of the Earth stops for about 24 hours. Geologists and scientists may not agree with my hypothesis but which terrible devastation they expect when the rotation stopped was already happened on the North African region. If the geologists start investigate this region in my hypothesis, they will arrive a conclusion about the catastrophe took place in this region in the near past.

What if the Sahara had not formed?

If the Sahara Desert had not formed, it would have had a notable impact on both the African content and Earth as a whole. This would become a global issue. The Sahara desert plays a crucial role in the climate and ecosystem of Africa and beyond.

Without the Sahara, the climate in the region would have been quite different, with potentially more moisture and vegetation. This would have affected the distribution of the people living in the area. That means every season there were lot of rains and flooding of the rivers all through the year.

On a global scale, the absence of the Sahara desert would have altered weather patterns and ocean currents, leading changes in regional and global climates. It might have influenced the atmospheric circulation and precipitation patterns across Africa and other parts of the world.

Overall, the non-existence of the Sahara desert would have had far reaching consequences for the African continent and the Earth's climate and ecosystems.

Significance of Rock art in Sahara

Rock art in the Sahara holds immense historical significance, providing valuable insights into the region's past and the population who inhabited it. Here is a glimpse of its time line in the desert's history. The geologists are going back to millions of years about the existence of the people in this region. If we observe closely the below data the nomads lived in this region just before 1405 BC.

The earliest known rock painting in the Sahara can be traced back to 12,000 BC-6,000 BC. These paintings are characterized by simple geometric designs and images of animals, showing the early societies reliance on hunting and gathering for sustenance. During Pastoral period 6,000BC- 2,000 BC rock art become more intricate and varied. Paintings depicted scenes of cattle herding and domestication, reflecting the growing importance of pastoralism as a way of life in the Sahara. Artistic styles evolved, showcasing more detailed depictions of animals and humans.

When we observe the above period, some rock arts reflected that up to 2000 BC the Green Sahara existed. The author claims that end of the green Sahara was 1405 BC which was very close to the pastoral period of the region.

As the author mentioned earlier the green Sahara ends in a single day and the North African lands became hot and sand dunes deposited in a single day and night. The mythical stories and the oral tradition reveals that something strange happened in this region abruptly and the North African region changed as desert and it was not possible to the mankind to reverse it. This spot in Western Africa became a marvellous structure and many assumptions and speculations being prevailed in this modern society.

CHAPTER ELEVEN
Radio Carbon dating

Carbon-14 dating also known as Radiocarbon dating is a method used to determine the age of organic material. It relies on the fact that Carbon-14, an isotope of carbon, is present in the atmosphere and taken in by living organisms. When an organism dies, it no longer takes in carbon-14 and the existing carbon-14 in its body begins to decay. By measuring the remaining carbon-14 in a sample, scientists can estimate its age. This method is commonly used in archaeology, anthropology and geology to date organic artifacts and remains.

Carbon-14 dating has some limitations and potential source of error that scientists take into account when analysing results. When the sample is contaminated with carbon from a different source or if it has been exposed to modern carbon, it can lead to inaccurate outcomes.

The carbon-14 dating method relies on the assumption that the atmospheric carbon-14 levels have remained relatively constant over time. Any fluctuations in atmospheric carbon-14 levels can affect the accuracy of the dating method. The size and quality of the sample can impact the accuracy of carbon-14 dating. Smaller or poorly preserved samples may provide less reliable results.

All the organic matter deposited in Sahara desert was exposed to high temperatures and mixed with the carbon came out of the mantle of the Earth. We all know that the matter from mantle should eventually dates to millions of years, because this matter existed inside the Earth from the time they were dating back. The main hypothesis of this book is that the entire North African region exposed to high temperature and scorched by the heat of the hot sand poured upon it.

The half-life of carbon-14 is approximately 5,730 years. However, this value can vary slightly in different environments. Corrections are made based on known values, but small variations can still introduce errors. Interpreting carbon-14 dating results requires consideration of other factors, such as the potential for carbon exchange reservoir effects and fluctuations in carbon-14 levels in different organisms.

When the organic matter subjects to high temperatures, how does it affect the carbon dating?

When organic matter is subjected to high temperatures, such as being scorched by heavy heat, it can affect the carbon-14 dating process in several ways.

High temperatures can cause organic material to lose carbon through processes like combustion or volatilization. This can result in a loss of carbon-14 in the sample, making it appear older than it would be.

Heat can also cause carbon to exchange with the surrounding environment. This can introduce modern carbon into the sample or remove older carbon, leading to inaccurate dating results. Extreme heat can alter the isotope composition of carbon in the samples, which can affect the ratio of carbon-14 to stable carbon isotopes. This can complicate the dating process and lead to incorrect age estimates.

Heating organic material can make it more susceptible to contamination with modern carbon from the environment. Contaminants introduced during or after the scorching process can affect the accuracy of the carbon-14 dating results. High temperatures can also affect the structural integrity of the organic material being dated. Charred or burned samples may be more fragile and prone to contamination of the dating process.

Exposing organic matter to heavy heat can significantly impact the reliability of carbon-14 dating by altering the content introducing contaminants and affecting the isotopic composition of sample.

Dear readers, the author is requesting everyone to examine the all aspects in this book carefully. The North African lands were subjected to heavy heat in 1405 BC as the sand with fire poured on the region and severe heat waves devastated the region as the rotation of the Earth partially stopped. The junctions of the four tectonic plates were wide open, the lava, sand and fire poured upon the North African lands devastated every grass lands, wood savannahs and the woods on every hill and mountain in this region. When we observe the mountain ranges of the region it is evident that every hill and mountain was scorched by severe heat in 1405 BC. The carbon dating may differ to the above mentioned date because organic compounds came into contact with heavy heat conditions. The lava poured on a spot in the Mauritania region then this spectacular Eye of the Sahara formed as the molten lava and sand poured upon this region. The junctions of tectonic plates which were relatively near to West African region in 1405 BC. Due to heavy pressure in the mantle of the Earth, huge amounts of sand with fire burst out and poured upon the western Africa and very high heat waves travelled across the North African lands and made this great devastation possible on the face of the earth. So we cannot rely on the data of carbon dating of the rocks and other fossils in this region.

CHAPTER TWELVE

Conclusion

This is an unexpected book from my pen. I authored a book "Joshua's Long Day @ American Tectonic Plate Movements" in 2016 while I was searching for geological evidence for Joshua's Long Day in the geological history of the Earth. In my search, I found a sentence in Plato's writings, "Atlantis was deluged in a single day and night by fire and Tsunamis." This phrase flashed a light in my mind and read many books and found that Atlantis deluge was only possible with Tectonic Plate Movements, because Atlantis was at size of Asia Minor and Libya together. When I studied about Tectonic Plate Movements, North and South American tectonic plates were divergent and some other plates on earth were converging. When we observe the Atlantic ridge in mid- Atlantic Ocean it reveals that new ocean bed had been formed when the North, South American tectonic plates travelled westward with an unusual speed in 1405 BC.

Atlantis was a real place and it was deluged by Tectonic Plate Movements on Joshua's Long Day as Joshua prayed for extra day light in Israel. The Sun and Moon stayed above the Middle East means these two tectonic plates should be static for about a day. Hence, I confirmed the Arabian and African tectonic plate's static about a day and when the junctions of North, South American tectonic plates and African, Eurasian Plates wide open lava travelled just like a projectile and poured upon a spot helping this spectacular structure formation i.e., Eye of the Sahara. On the same day the North, South American Tectonic Plates travelled west ward with unusual speed reaching present positions in single day and night. Tilt of the Earth supported this incident and the North, south American Plates travelled westward with unusual speed. This mystery was clearly explained in my previous title "Joshua's Long Day @

American Tectonic Plate Movements." Many do not believe my assumption of tectonic Plate movements by comparing the present speed of the plates as few centimetres per year. I proposed of tilt of the Earth on the same day because the supreme power on nature wants to give final Earth (final arrangements of continents) with settled tectonic plates and continents for the modern scientific society as on today.

During further research, I found a fact about Eye of the Sahara or Richat Structure being considered as geological wonder which can be observed from space and with the help of drone cameras. At present many theories and assumptions regarding formation of this structure are running. I wonder if some are assuming that this was lost civilization, Atlantis. It is no way to compare this structure with Atlantis because Plato mentioned it as an island and with a big size of Asia Minor and Libya together. Presently, some are proposing it was formed by meteorite collision because of the stones that appear on the site. But neither volcanic nor meteorite activity present on this site. The circular formation with rhyolite and sandstone presence because of the lava came out of the mantle through the junctions of Tectonic plates. The high pressure of the inner earth (in giga Pascals) made it possible to travel long distance from Atlantic Ocean just like a projectile and poured upon a spot while the Arabian, African plates stood still for about a day. Please remember that Atlantis was close to the west Africa before 1405 BC.

Enormous heat waves prevailed at that time and scorched the entire North African continent in a single day and night. Afterwards the deposited sand spread across the lands and the rotation of the Earth resumed as usual after Joshua's long day.

First of all, I appreciate with all my heart all the geologists, climatologists and researchers who spent their valuable time researching about the mystery of Sahara Desert. In fact when I watched many documentaries on Sahara I knew how difficult it was to make all these videos. But I must say that the geologists were in error in estimating the age of the Sahara. This land was scorched by terrible heat and then by a Mega Tsunami, means overflowing the Atlantic Ocean into the North African lands. Recently I watched a video on YouTube titled, "Sahara's Hidden Catastrophe: Investigating the Mega tsunami Hypothesis. This video suggests that mega tsunami from Mediterranean and North Atlantic hit the North African region in an unprecedented way. Once I read about millions of tons of mud accumulated along the Atlantic ridge which made it very difficult to excavate the ocean to unearth the Atlantis in the depths of Atlantic Ocean. Please remember that mud in the ocean is evidence for volcanic activity along the junctions of tectonic plates and a proof to our hypothesis.

Why this great devastation in this field? We may conclude that it was very difficult to travel tectonic plates at high speed. What happened to ancient city Pompeii in Rome? Even in this historic period of 79 AD, how did the volcano devastate the entire city within hours? Even though in many cases the volcanic activity starts slowly and ends in months or even years. Excavations are still on going to understand what happened to this city. We have many unanswered questions about this incident.

I propose another reason for this devastation. I mentioned giant king Atlas ruled Atlantis arrogantly and their belief system is quite different from the other humans. The king Atlas is giant and propagated that he was the king of the universe and humiliates the race of Noah in all occasions. My previous title explains fully why these giants behaved like that. As Atlantis was at a navigable distance from Western Africa before 1405 BC, this false belief system also spread into the North African region. We have experienced the panic of end of the world on Dec 21, 2012. The origin of this belief system was Atlantis. The people lived in Central America proposed the calendar which was Mayan calendar. The world did not end up on Dec 21, 2012. This is the example of the belief system of hybrid race of Atlantis in that pre-historic period.

In order to share what my spirit is prompting me about some issues on the face of the Earth, I authored this book "Eye of the Sahara @ Plate Tectonics". I believe the word "God" is eternal and the history of the Bible is a fact if you believe it or not. I request every reader to investigate into my claim and come to an outcome that the Eye of the Sahara which was a geological wonder of the Earth. I request the reader to go through the available articles being published endlessly to explain formation of formation of Eye of the Sahara.

In certain day of 1405 BC the below geological occurrences were happened and we should see all of them collectively:

1. Atlantis Deluge in a single day and night
2. Westward spreading of North, South American Tectonic Plates in 24 hours
3. Pouring out of lava from the plate junctions on a spot in western Africa forming Eye of the Sahara at Mauritania
4. Pouring out of sand and fire from the junctions in a day on the North African lands in a massive way.
5. Sun and Moon stood still in Middle East on Joshua's long day
6. Tilt of the Earth about 23.5 degrees east on this very day.
7. Mega Tsunami from Atlantic Ocean devastated the North African region

The stone formation at the Eye of the Sahara clearly taught us that these rocks were connected with volcanic activity and molten rock deposits formed at once making circular shape with a diameter of 40-50 km. This was possible only because the lava poured from the sky out of mantle of the earth. We know that the pressure inside the Earth was very high and measured in giga Pascal and the powerful convection currents of lava inside the Earth made it possible to form a structure which looks like an Eye from the space.

Interestingly until 1960s, this area was like mere hill ranges and many nomads lived there and prepared some weapons with metals known at that time. Anyhow, this formation was like a bull's Eye gazing at space was seen from the space and got the name as Eye of the Sahara and remain as evidence of geological incident occurred in the history of mankind.

Dear reader, these are the days mankind critical towards the word of God is increasing, but the word is eternal and entire Bible is a treasure of mysteries and never gives full evidence to satisfy human mind and theories.

If the library in Alexandria had not burned up, then we would have some more evidence of these catastrophes on record. The only record available was Plato's mention of Atlantis in the dialogues Timaeus and Critia. This dialogue gave a little light about the deluge of Atlantis. As I am a believer in the word of God, I gave my best to link up these 7 incidents mentioned above with Joshua's Long Day in the Biblical history. So read my book with faith in God and examine the reasons given in this book, you will know His unaltered power on the Earth as he is the King, Creator of the Earth.

Bibliography

* The Holy Bible
* Tectonic Plate Theory from Internet
* Smithsonian Magazine
* Phaethon and His story from Internet
* Joshua's long Day @ American Tectonic plate Movements
* IFLSCIENCE weekly Newsletter
* Magazine Geographical and many videos and printed articles in social media.

SPECIAL CHAPTER

This chapter clarifies how the span of 3 days and 3 nights extends from Friday to Sunday morning of Jesus death and resurrection.

JONAH'S SIGN

JESUS CHRIST'S RESURRECTION @3 DAYS & 3 NIGHTS

Now-a-days many believers and even servants of God misled into understanding certain Biblical truths. In the beginning there was Word. That Word was God. The Word of God is God himself for the Christians. That is why we have to continue to study the word of God till we get proper revelation from God. We can understand certain Biblical truths only with the help of the Holy Spirit. So we should not be in a hash to unravel the mystery with our own worldly wisdom. There are many subjects like that and I am trying to bring one of them to attention.

There are many servants of God, believers and church leaders who are confused about the truth of the Lord's resurrection after 3 days and 3 nights after being buried.

In Matthew 12: 38-40, the scripture says, "Then some of the Pharisees and teachers of the law said to him, "Teacher, we want to see a sign from above, He answered, "A wicked and adulterous generation asks for a miraculous sign! But none will be given it except the sign of the prophet Jonah. For as Jonah was three days and three nights in the belly of a huge fish, so the Son of Man will be three days and three nights in the heart of the earth." (NIV)

Here there are three nights and three days = 36 +36 = 72 hours (3 days and 3 nights) in the reckoning . But Lord Jesus' death took place between Friday 3:00 P.M. and Saturday 3:00 P.M. which comes to 24 hrs. Saturday 3:00 P.M. to Sunday morning 3:00 A.M. it is another 12 hrs. So it comes to a total 36 hrs. Then what about the remaining 36 hours ? Let us now think about it carefully.

First of all we must understand that Jesus Christ was born into this world as a human being. That is what the Bible is teaching us. So we have to, first of all, have proper understanding of man's creation.

Man = Spirit + Soul + Body

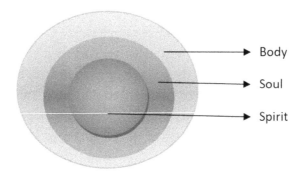

In case of an ordinary human being's death (fallen man's) , the soul and spirit will be imprisoned in Hades. We believe that Jesus Christ was born into this world as a son of man to save mankind and to redeem the soul and the spirit of man from hell. We see in Isaiah 61:1 how the Lord Jesus Christ was manifested as the one who declared freedom to the captive as one of many of His works in this world.

The physical body of Jesus Christ is holy and sinless. That is why Psalmist David says that the Lord's body was not decomposed. His soul was holy and without sin and it was all powerful.

His spirit was also so holy that it can be equated with God's Spirit or Holy Spirit.

In the Gospel, according to St. John, in chapter 19:30, in Matthew 27:50 and in Luke 23:46 the same incident was recorded. It said, " Jesus called out with a loud voice, "Father, into your hands I commit my spirit."

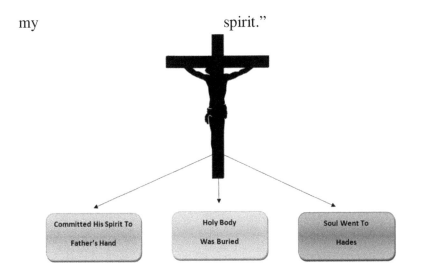

Till Jesus was crucified, the soul and spirit of the Old Testament saints were in hades. This fact is the Biblical truth and it can be proved by so many Bible verses. In Genesis 42:38 Jacob said "My son will not go down with you; his brother is died and he is the only one left. If harm comes to him on the journey you are taking, you will being my grey head down to the grave (in Hebrew it is Sheol) in sorrow. In Genesis 44: 29 the same thing is mentioned.

However, we have scriptural evidences to prove the fact that both the places, Paradise and Hades was in the uttermost part of the earth separated from each other until the death of Jesus on the cross of Calvary.

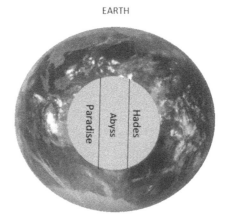

We do not know exactly the locations of Paradise and Hades inside the earth. But we know that both the places Paradise and hades were in prison under the earth according to the Old and New Testament texts.

As the Old Testament saints were not completely redeemed, paradise was still kept under the earth. This was because the death of Jesus on the cross did not yet taken place. The redemption price for the Old Testament saints was not yet paid. They were under collective bondage.

Prophesying about the life of Jesus Christ, prophet Isaiah says in 61:1; "The spirit of the Sovereign Lord is on me, because the Lord has anointed me to preach good news to the poor. He has sent me to bind up the broken hearted, to proclaim freedom for the captives and release from darkness for the prisoners". (NIV)

So, the Lord sent his son for this purpose. In St. Paul's letter to Ephesians 4: 8-9,St. Paul says "When he ascended on high, he led captives in his train and gave gifts to men. What does 'he ascended' mean except that he also descended to the lower earthly regions? ".

By the death and resurrection of Jesus Christ, Satan's power has been annulled and his spirit world has been destroyed. Explaining the same subject St. Paul says in his letter to Colossians 2:15, "And having disarmed the powers and authorities, he made a public spectacle of them, triumphing over them by the cross" (NIV).

Though the Christian world, especially the born- again Christian believers undergo pain and sorrow over the Lord's sufferings and crucifixion, the blood he shed on the cross has brought salvation to all the Old Testament and New Testament saints.

In Mathew 27:50-53, we see how the Lord Jesus Christ separated Paradise from Hades. The scripture says"And when Jesus had cried out again in a loud voice, he gave up his spirit at that moment the curtain of the temple was torn in two from top to bottom. The earth shook and the rocks split. The tombs broke open and the bodies of many holy people who had died were raised to life. They came out of the tombs, and after Jesus resurrection they went into the holy city and appeared to many people"(NIV).

How powerful is the Soul of the Lord Jesus Christ! As soon as Jesus died on Friday and as His powerful Soul went to Hades, there was redemption granted to "Abraham's blossom". However, only Jesus is the first fruit of the resurrected saints. As there is no body from Adam to Malchai who is powerful in soul and spirit, the Almighty came into this world as Jesus Christ and removed the fear of death in mankind through death. The scripture says " Since the children have flesh and blood, he too shared in their humanity so that by his death he might destroy him who holds the power of death – that is, the devil and free those who all their lives were held in slavery by their fear of death." Hebrew 2:14-15 (NIV).

Then how can we explain the concept of three nights and three days meaning $36 + 36= 72$ hours. First we must understand that Lord Jesus Christ's 'Soul' is living and a powerful . There is no death either to his soul or spirit. But the body was dead and buried. As Jesus' soul was living, that time must be considered (in earthly language) as DAY only. At the same time, it was declared by Roman soldiers that

Jesus died on the cross. And later, his body was buried in the tomb of Joseph. So, that time must be considered as night.

Though dead, Jesus living soul spent 36 hrs in Hades. At the same time, his body was resting in the tomb for 36 hrs. So it comes to 72 hrs. which constitute 3 days and 3 nights.

The following diagram illustrates this truth further:

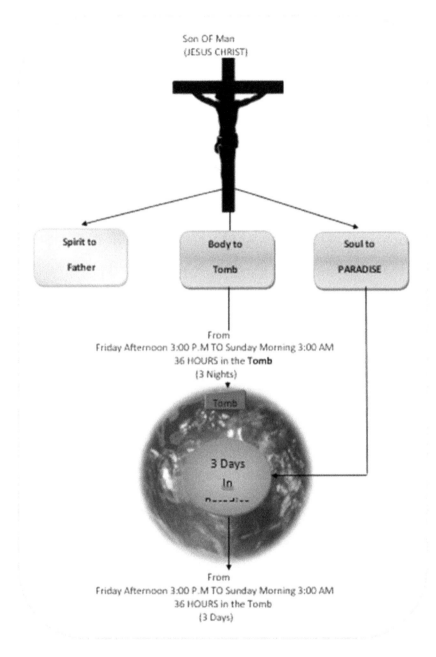

In the above matter '36 HOURS in the Tomb' to be replaced by " 36 HOURS in the Paradise"

We may get a doubt that from Friday 3:00 P.M to Sunday morning 3:00 A.M there were days and nights together passed away, how can we take that time as night? But for a person who is dead, the whole time i.e., 36 hours will be **night** only. Since there is no difference of day and night to the dead bodies and at the same time we should not forget that the soul of Jesus Christ was so powerful and full of life that went into Paradise to bring out the imprisoned souls from there. As the working time is always considered as day, we are considering that time of 36 hrs as **day** only.

So our thinking must change towards the living and unchanging word of God. May God help us to take his word as infallible. You are free to consult the author if you have any doubts with regard to the explanation to this write-up.

The author believes that this truth is clear to your spirit and mind. If you agree with me, praise God as he revealed this truth to a meek and weak vessel in these last days. Please read the below carefully and respond to this request.

I have authored a book called 'Paradise Found', to reveal the secret of the location of Garden of Eden in Israel itself. I authored and published this book in U.S.A with much strain and spending lot of money, because this issue was a challenge to both Christians and non-Christians as well. It was a mystery for the last 6,000 years. This mystery revealed through this book. Therefore, I request to order this book and read it and post your feedback.

Contact info:
Anipe Steeven King VPJ B.Sc;B.Ed;M.Div.
1-3-49/1, Pension Line
SAMALKOT-533440
Kakinada Dt, Andhra Pradesh
Cell:91-807487143,91-9493050992
e-mail: victorprem.vpc@gmail.com

Books Published

Paradise Found

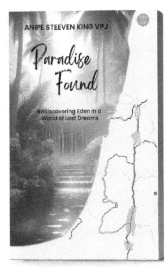

Paradise 'Garden of Eden' lost due to the sin and disobedience of first Adam. This was a big loss to the entire human race. This Paradise was missed from the earth and history. This was a hidden mystery from the beginning. There is an answer for every problem if we can delve into the Bible. Where was the Garden of Eden? This was the challenging issue to every Christian and non-Christian. The prominent 17th century poet narrated the story of 'Paradise Lost' through his poetry. But we do not know actual location of the Paradise.

God revealed this mystery to his servant and the Paradise was Found in Israel itself. Are you wish to know the location of the "Garden of Eden" on the face of the earth?. Please come with me by reading the God revealed truth about lost Paradise, then you can found it on the earth geographically and also you will agree with me. Praise the Lord, the Paradise was Found. Those who lost the Paradise in their hearts, please read this book diligently, you can restore it by the Spirit of God.

" But thou art cast forth away from thy sepulcher like an abominable branch, clothed with the slain, that are thrust through with the sword, that go down to the stones of the pit; as a dead body trodden under foot." Isaiah 14:19 (ASV).

Dead body mentioned in this scripture is nothing but 'Dead Sea'. This was proven through this book.

As mentioned in the above scriptures Isaiah 14:19 Lord God trampled the fallen spirits into the pit through the Garden of Eden region during the Flood. All the details given through the graphics and maps you can easily understand this revelation. If you find difficulty in your first reading, please go one more round. I believe that the Spirit of God help you to understand this book. Please post your opinion about this book.

Yours

Anipe Steeven King VPJ B.Sc; B.Ed; M.Div

Author, Paradise Found

Email: victorprem.vpc@gamil.com,

91-8074871493

Joshua's Long Day@ American Tectonic Plate Movements

A prominent 3rd Century (BC) Philosopher narrated the story of Atlantis and used a phrase' it was destroyed in single day and night'. When the author was searching for physical evidence on earth for the miracle of Joshua's Long day, this phrase became a base in the space of historical speculations about this occurrence. It is not possible to be missed a continent in a single day and night. It was only possible with tectonic plate movements in the Atlantic Ocean:

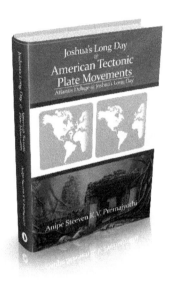

- There was a link between Atlantis deluge and Joshua's Long day.
- Atlantis was deluged by tectonic plate movements in Atlantic Ocean.
- Central American region was at navigable distance to Atlantis prior to 1405 BC.
- North & South American Plates diverged and Nazca and cocoos plates sub ducted.
- Sea Floor spreading was occurred in mid Atlantic ridge.
- African and Arabian plates stand stood for about a day i.e Joshua's Long Day.
- American Plates travelled with unusual speed – terrible tsunamis and earthquakes hit the land of Atlantis and around Mediterranean Sea.
- There were many long day and long night (other side) occurrences recorded.

Above points discussed in detail in this book. The people of Atlantis belonged to Bronze age . Many evidences given to support this view. Many books and researches of noble persons helped to come to a comfortable conclusion Atlantis Deluge @ American Tectonic Plate Movements.

This book is available in amazon and flipkart.

Yours
Anipe Steeven King VPJ B.Sc; B.Ed; M.Div
Author, Paradise Found
Email: victorprem.vpc@gamil.com,
918074871493